Take Nothing for Granted

Take Nothing for Granted

Tales from an Unexpected Life

Ross Kemp

SEVEN DIALS

First published in Great Britain in 2023 by Seven Dials,
an imprint of The Orion Publishing Group Ltd
Carmelite House, 50 Victoria Embankment
London EC4Y 0DZ

An Hachette UK Company

1 3 5 7 9 10 8 6 4 2

A CIP catalogue record for this book is
available from the British Library.

ISBN (Hardback) 978 1 3996 0972 2
ISBN (eBook) 978 1 3996 0974 6
ISBN (Audio) 978 1 3996 0975 3

Typeset by Born Group
Printed and bound in Great Britain by Clays Ltd, Elcograf S.p.A.

www.orionbooks.co.uk

For my family

Contents

Introduction

There's a very specific noise a bullet makes when it flies past your head. The whistling, swishing sound of air being displaced by a small piece of extremely hot metal travelling at twice the speed of sound. If you hear that noise they're usually not missing by much. As we scrambled for cover, I found myself wondering, not for the first time over the years, if perhaps acting hadn't been so bad after all.*

My crew and I threw ourselves to the floor, sheltering behind whatever we could on the exposed rooftop in Lyari, a notorious region of Karachi. We were there to meet Uzair Baloch, one of the most wanted men in Pakistan, for a series of films we were making about parts of the world where extreme events were occurring. Baloch was either a freedom fighter or a murderer, depending on who you talked to. Earlier in the afternoon, we had spent time with him walking around Lyari as he waved to the crowds who were calling out his name like he was a pop star. Then there were reports that the paramilitary force known as the Pakistan Rangers were moving in and we went up to the roof to try and get a better view and that's where I was stood between Baloch and the cameraman when the shooting started.†

---

* Recently, I've gone back to acting and I love it.

† Sorry, Mum. I'm always trying to reassure her that what I'm doing won't be dangerous and not to worry. Her response is: 'I've had to worry about you since the day you were born.'

1

I've been shot at quite a lot over the years. When we were making films in Afghanistan it was not uncommon to have five or six contacts with the enemy before 8 in the morning. You can get used to being shot at and it not feeling personal. But this felt *very* personal.

We scrambled off the roof and into a saferoom on the ground floor, where we watched as the news reported that Baloch had killed members of the British media and that government forces were preparing to move in and capture him. He tried to reassure us that he would never shoot us.[*]

There was a tense stand-off as we made it clear we *really* needed to leave before the police raided and our hosts tried to decide if it might be better to have us around if they did. Then the lights went out. What you're supposed to do when this happens is lie face down in the corner of the room, so you're not hit by the explosion when the police blast their way in. What you're not supposed to do is pull out a cigarette lighter and do a piece to camera saying, 'They've cut the power.' I've never been very good at following instructions.[†]

Finally, after the sun had set and we'd paid our driver extra danger money, we were smuggled down a side road and made our way to relative safety on the outskirts of Lyari. The director caught my eye and said, 'Leaving shot?' We were all still pretty shaken from our narrow escape, but we agreed we needed something to end the sequence.

I set off down one end of the alley on my own, so I could come walking back and do my piece to camera. Then a tuk-tuk started coming slowly down the dark alleyway. I froze. This

---

[*] Which is one of those things that isn't actually that reassuring to hear someone say.

[†] I was the same with toys on Christmas morning and still am.

was at a time when everyone was on incredibly high alert for shootings and kidnappings, as they were happening so often. Then, at the end of the alley, it turned back around and pulled level with me as I was walking. Typical. We'd survived the roof, only for me to be gunned down in a back alley. I held my breath as it drew level with me.

Out of the corner of my eye I saw a shadowy arm raise and level something at my head. And as I turned, there was a sudden flash of light. I heard in a loud and unmistakably Brummie accent:

'Are you Grant Mitchell?!' Then a giggle.

Time is a funny thing. It rhymes and echoes. Things from your past find their way into your present, things you experience suddenly help you make sense of your past. When I was a kid, I used to pretend that the scrubland, woods and irrigation ditches in the fields next to my house in Essex were the Amazon rainforest, swinging a stick and imagining it was a machete. Thirty years later I found myself travelling through the Amazon, using a real one. I've spent the years in between telling stories, first as an actor, then for the last twenty years making documentaries in some of the most extraordinary places in the world.

I've been fed cake by Nazis on three continents.* Set on fire by them once in Moscow. I've got accidentally engaged (and very quickly unengaged) to a gang leader's sister in El Salvador. I've had poison oak spat at me by one of Michael Jackson's elephants. I've been farted on by the Taliban. I've been threatened with spears, shot at more times than I can

_____

* I don't know why Nazis love cake so much. I can only assume when you're all about putting your symbols and insignia on things, the clean expanse of a freshly iced cake is impossible to resist.

remember with rockets, bullets and one time by twelve-inch nails dipped in faeces and frog poison.

I've shared a beer with men capable of the most extreme violence and found myself warming to them. I've listened to a people trafficker tell me he'd killed at least four hundred girls and known that killing him would make the world a better place. I've come as close to evil as I ever want to go and seen the most extraordinary kindness and bravery human beings are capable of. I've been to fifty-three countries and seen aspects of Britain I could never have imagined. I've been in too many morgues and prisons.

Through it all I will always be grateful that I once played that role in an iconic television show that still gets me recognised halfway around the world more than twenty-five years later. It would later turn out the woman in the tuk-tuk had recently moved from Birmingham to live with her husband in Karachi and what she'd raised at my head was her mobile phone to take a photo; she then asked if we could take a selfie, which I agreed to, she was a very kind lady and we talked for a while.

Through it all, there's been no plan. No map. No strategy. I've gone where the next interesting thing was and never quite fitted neatly into any box.

I've had a career drawn towards men and violence, but it's been strong women who have shaped my life. From my mum and the Essex matriarchs whose hair she cut, the strong East End women, epitomised by Barbara Windsor, who I was surrounded by for a decade on set, to the extraordinary brave women who have put their lives at risk to help us make our films and now, my wife. When I think about my life, it's not the hard men I think about, but the women I have seen who bend and somehow do not break.

4

People often ask me when I've been most scared – was it when I had guns and spears pointed at me in Papua New Guinea, or meeting murderers, or when the bullets were whistling around my head in Afghanistan, and I think it's actually that moment when you wake up in the middle of the night overcome by the fear that maybe you won't always be there for your kids, you won't always be able to fix everything and keep them safe. That they have to go out and live their own lives. At some point they're going to go out into the world and fall in love, and have their heart broken and feel homesick and lost and alone.* Without the risk of that, you wouldn't get to have the joy and the love and the happiness. Because of what I've seen, I'm very much aware of how fragile life is and I have that in mind every time I kiss them goodbye.

I was the sort of kid it was easy to give up on at school till I found rugby and acting. I was the Essex boy at drama school, who didn't quite fit in, playing rugby in the morning and dancing to New Romantic music at night. I played a famous fictional hardman on TV for a decade, but have spent twice as long making films about some of the genuinely hardest places on the planet. I've got myself into and out of scrapes and scraps. I've spent time in bedsits and on superyachts, eaten in luxury restaurants with some of the most powerful people on the planet, and in slums with some of the poorest people in the world.

These are the stories of some of the things that have happened to me along the way: the funny things, the scary things, the exciting things: the things that have made me who I am. I don't want to start at the beginning and tell them

---

* Honestly, they need to invent a new word for that feeling of being a parent – that precise mixture of extreme joy and terror.

in chronological order because that's not the way my brain works. And this certainly isn't going to be one of those books full of life lessons – though I'm almost sixty and I've had some experiences along the way that I've certainly learned from.* It's likely there will be a useful list of things *not* to do by the end of this book.

I've always been curious about people – how they move, how they talk, how they act and why – it's been the thread that connects being an actor and making the sorts of films I do. I've always been passionate about finding and telling stories.

And now, for the first time, here are mine.

---

* For example: if you're going to get run over by your girlfriend, in your own car, in the process of splitting up with her, try and make sure it's a model that's low to the ground so you go right over the top.

A Brief Interlude

Before we get going, there are some things you need to know. (Think of it as that bit before a film where they ask you to put your phone on silent.)

Working on this book involved collecting a lot of stories from the past, many of which involve exciting things happening to me in dangerous places. But I want you to know that's not really my life now.* My life now is chaos of a very different sort. My wife, Renée, our eight-year-old son and my five-year-old twin daughters, my son from a previous relationship who I see at weekends and Bruno our Golden Retriever. My days now are a blur of pick-ups and drop-offs, of playdates and school uniforms, of little pieces of cut up fruit and vegetables in boxes and reminders on the kitchen blackboard. Of laughter and shrieking and that pause as the adults wait to see if that was a good shriek or a bad one.

Having young kids when you're a bit older has its ups and downs. Everything aches. But hopefully you have more patience. I'm pretty sure I couldn't have done it when I was younger. Having a family is a constant reminder that you're not the centre of the universe. It's hard to be too up yourself when you're being critiqued for bringing 'the wrong socks' in

---

* You should also know I drink a lot less now. Honestly reading a lot of this back, my liver winces.

the morning, or for not cleaning the kitchen floor properly. It's hard to believe your own hype when you're trapped, like a giant deranged glove puppet, shrieking in fury as you try and put the duvet in the duvet cover. When you're outnumbered by your children, just do the maths. If all of them decide to run in a different direction at the same time, it's checkmate.

My wife, Renée, is an incredibly organised person and is a corporate lawyer. When we first met, she was due to go back to Australia to take up a partnership and for some reason, that I'll be eternally grateful for, she decided to stay with me in the UK.* Renée had never seen *EastEnders*. She got to know me as this guy that goes off regularly to these far-flung places. And to be honest, she probably got used to having a bit of a break from me. I still plan on making the sorts of documentaries I find interesting, so I'm sure I'll be off somewhere again at some point. Until then, like a lot of people, a big chunk of my life seems to be videocalls, which when they're not muted so I can referee something with the kids, involve trying to guess if someone is frozen or if that's just their paying attention face.

I suppose what I'm trying to say is that sometimes I'm watching TV and I wonder – does Dwayne 'The Rock' Johnson know where the dishwasher salt goes?

I do know where it goes, by the way. While I was working on these stories of bullets flying around me, I was also mopping up after Bruno, my dog, who is at a stage in his life where he frequently doesn't make it outside in time. I was hoovering. Or, I was loading and unloading the dishwasher (because no one else can do it properly, though that's an ongoing debate). The one thing I draw the line at is ironing, as I'm truly bad at

---

* Though believe me, it gets mentioned every time it rains.

it and I hate it so much. I look at all of the things that have happened and can't quite believe they all happened to me.

A book like this can't help but make you look at all the different yous there have been at different points. All those differently shaped lives. But if someone asked me which one was my favourite, I would say this one.

Formaldehyde

It could be a right pain having a copper for a dad. There was no point in lying, he'd just look at you and he'd *know*. It didn't stop me and my brother trying, of course – about how the window got broken, or the daffodils trampled – but he'd just keep looking at you not saying anything until you told him what had happened. And something had usually happened. Until I was eleven, I grew up in one of the last houses on a close in Rainham in Essex, right on the Thames Estuary.* People forget now how close the seventies were to the Second World War. There were still air raid shelters in back gardens, over-grown bomb sites to explore if you climbed the right fences. Most of our granddads had fought in the war, almost all of our dads had done national service. My dad served in the infantry and then military intelligence. We'd spend hours high in the wooden frames of the houses they were building. The war was constantly there, in the toys we wanted, in the games we played. I remember being obsessed with a die-cast metal model of a Spitfire the boy across the road had, but we didn't have the money for it at that time. So my poor mum bought me a different plastic one. I can still see her face in the bedroom window as she threw it down to get me excited

---

* Interesting fact, it's about half an inch to the right of where the Thames is cropped off on the *EastEnders* map.

about it: 'Look, this one can actually fly.' But I was utterly graceless in that way kids can be. It was the wrong one. It's only when you become a parent that you understand just how that must have felt. I got it for Christmas, but I learned that you couldn't always have everything you wanted in the order you wanted it.

It was in many ways a classic seventies childhood: choppers and space hoppers, sherbet Dip Dabs and fizzy Corona orange. No wonder we were hyper. There was a little gang of us, the first gang in my life, John Barratt, Martin Gracy, all with younger brothers. The Abbot Close Gang. We'd kick balls through windows and ride about on our bikes, recreating what we'd seen on the TV that week – imagining our bikes were horses and the sticks were lances, making a knight's helmet out of the cardboard box the ice creams came in. Or we were cowboys, or musketeers, but a lot of the time we were Second World War soldiers. We'd disappear onto the scrubland for entire days fighting wars. We'd go out onto the marshes and come back plastered in stinking mud. We'd be back on the close, throwing mud grenades, clasping our hand to our chests from the bullets, making machine-gun noises. All while the woman in the house opposite us flicked her Venetian blinds and called out, 'I can see what you're up to and I'll tell your mum and dad.'* It was rough and tumble. We'd get into fights with other gangs from different closes. One day I came back from an adventure where we'd decided to recreate news

---

* I went back to the close while I was working on this book to try and shake some memories loose and a woman came out of her house and watched me intently for a bit before telling me she knew my dad was a copper. When I confirmed he was, she closed the door. No cup of tea. It was like I'd never been away.

footage of riots in Northern Ireland by throwing broken bits of slate roofing tile at each other and one had cut my brother's head. I was about eight years old and must have used the f-word, at which point my mum washed my mouth out with Imperial Leather soap as my brother bled on the carpet.*

My brother and I, like all brothers, had our disagreements as kids, frequently, but we made a good team when we needed to.

Like the time we'd been told we weren't allowed to go fishing at this specific lake we'd heard about because it was too far away and we were too young. I must have been eleven and he was about nine. We decided we were going to go anyway, secretly.

We go to the fishing tackle shop and buy a pint of maggots each in preparation.† We're told that they can't be too hot or too cold, or they won't wriggle enough to catch the eye of the fish. So we need to find somewhere indoors to hide them. And maggots stink. Which means we need to find somewhere to hide them where Mum won't find them. So we hide them in the spare room, which was the room my nan and granddad sleep in when they stay with us. Then we sneak out and put our rods on our bikes.

In the morning, we get up at 5 a.m., while it's still dark, whispering and on tiptoes. And go to retrieve our two pints of maggots. Only there's not two pints of maggots. There's one pint of maggots and one empty box where a pint of maggots used to be. And then I see out of the corner of my eye that

---

* Sadly it didn't work and I still let myself down with the occasional swear word.

† I don't know who is in charge of this stuff but I'd like to lobby for a unit of maggots other than pints.

the bedroom carpet is moving. Then I see that the eiderdown on the bed is moving. There are maggots crawling everywhere. Leaving aside the issue of who didn't put the lid back on their pint of maggots, we leap into action, picking up handfuls of maggots and putting them into the box. Then we leave the house before anyone is up, spend the day fishing and no one is any the wiser. We got away with it.

A couple of days later and that room is like something out of a horror film, swarming with bluebottles everywhere.

'Do either of you boys know anything about this?' asked Mum, and we just shook our heads. She must have known but she didn't tell Dad.

I absolutely loved television. *Thunderbirds* and *Captain Scarlet*, all the adventure shows. But my favourite was a show called *The Banana Splits*, which was a mixture of animation and these live-action segments with people dressed up in giant animal costumes. And one of the cartoons was *The Three Musketeers*, so that all went into the mix. We'd be musketeers shouting 'en garde' to each other, hitting each other with sticks. We'd pull everything we saw on the television into the games we played.

At the end of the close there was a hawthorn bush that had grown up into an arch, and some of the girls and I would hang one of my mum's eiderdowns up and have a little theatre. It was down where the ice-cream van would stop, so there was always an abundant supply of ice lolly sticks, which I would snap in two, sharpen on the edge of the kerb and insert them into my top lip as Dracula fangs and perform as a vampire.* 'I'm coming to get you,' I would shout and the girls would pretend

---

* My rate at that time was 1p per performance, or some Opal Fruits, which, as my agent will tell you, basically hasn't changed.

to faint. That was where I first learned about something called kissing, which was fun in a different way to hitting each other with bits of wood, though it felt equally dangerous.

'Wait till your father gets home' was a commonly heard refrain but it had a little extra to it in our case. As a detective, Dad kept us shielded from a lot of what went on. He worked long hours, was away for days at a time, and we never knew any details, just that it was serious stuff. At one point he was in the Flying Squad, the unit set up by Scotland Yard to deal with armed robbers, the proper gangsters. He carried a gun. Often he'd be back after my brother and I had gone to sleep and had left by the time we woke up, but he'd leave the empty cartridges on our headboards from when he'd been at the firing range. When I was little and about as tall as his kneecaps, I'd hug his legs when he got home, the feeling of the suit fabric against my face, the smell that was peculiar to him, a kind of faint chemical smell I didn't much like.

Dad had this brown leather suitcase with a brass lock and his initials embossed on it in gold and I was fascinated by it. I'd been told very clearly never to play with it or go anywhere near it. But every chance I got I'd go and look at it and play with the lock.

One day my dad was out and the case was there by the front door. I tried the lock and this time it was open. I remember knowing with absolute certainty that I shouldn't look in the case and that there would be repercussions. But, as has happened so often in my life, curiosity got the better of me.

Inside the case there were black-and-white photographs. I didn't know exactly what I was looking at but I knew it was a dead body and I knew something bad had happened. I put the photographs back in the case carefully, closed it

14

and put it back where it was. Didn't say anything to anyone. That evening when he got home, he came into the room, took one look at me and said, 'You've been in my case, haven't you?'

If my dad's gift was getting people to talk, my mum was a hairdresser and had that gift of being able to talk to anyone about anything. And she still does.* She'd often be cutting the hair of a neighbour when I got home from school. They'd be in there, the air thick with hairspray and dyes and the chemical peroxide scent of perm lotions, and women talking and laughing. Sometimes I'd sit in there too, listening, or they'd ask me to tell them about school or to do one of my impressions – Dick Emery, or *The Goodies* or *Dad's Army* – once they were out from under the dryer. People sitting and talking about their lives, exchanging stories. You leave a space and people fill it.

I wanted to be an actor as soon as I realised it was something you could be (and be paid for). That time was a real highpoint for television, it predominated and eclipsed everything. The quality was high. There were so few channels and the people who were involved were all good. Acting began with turning what we saw on the television into games. Then it was impressions of teachers. Then I got into school plays. But my teachers all said that my reading wasn't good enough to be an actor. I think now there's a much better sense of how different kids learn in different ways and at different paces. But back then it was that one size fits all model. Sit in a row as the teacher talks at you and writes things on the board. I couldn't get on with that and so I was labelled as not a high achiever and that was that. I was a bit of a loner at school when I was younger. But sport and then drama changed that.

---

* You don't need Wikipedia, just call Jean.

When I was eleven, we moved to a house in Shenfield in Essex. It was less than ten miles as the crow flies. But it was a huge shift in terms of those tiny markers of class we all grow up with. We went from the end of a close on a housing estate, to a house in the commuter belt. There were big gardens, and mock Tudor frontages. Our house was on a main road but backed onto some scrubby fields where I would range around with the dog imagining I was exploring far-off places. Our dog was a Hungarian Vizsla. He had literally been bred to accompany Hungarian aristocracy on hunts, and there he was being dragged around Essex scrubland; no wonder he had this permanent slightly wounded, disappointed air at what he was forced to endure.

The move marked the start of a new tradition too – the Sunday morning run with my dad. Dad had done his national service when he was younger and worked his way up from being a bobby on the beat. He believed that being able to run far and fast would always come in handy at some point in my life. So 8 a.m. on a Sunday, whatever the weather (though it felt like it was always raining), we'd put our nylon tracksuit bottoms on and our Gola football boots, the dog bounding around excitedly, and we'd run cross-country for a minimum of four miles, the cold air burning our lungs, until we collapsed in protest. 'Come on, boys!' he'd call back to us, laughing as we lay panting in the mud.*

As I got older, I used to go for runs out on the same waste ground our house backed on to. I used to do pull-ups on the trees. There was one particular tree that I used to climb

---

* There's been a few times where running quickly has literally saved my life. And it would come in handy when I started getting into playing rugby, which saved my life in a different way.

and build treehouses in, and I thought it would be a good idea to tie one end of a rope around one of the branches, the other around my chest, and see what happened when I jumped off.*

It was also where people would set fireworks off. So I would go around the next morning and I would collect any that hadn't gone off and scrape all of the powder into one. Then I'd light it. But this time there'd clearly been a lot that hadn't gone off and it went off like a bomb in my face and I was left lying on my back with the smell of singed hair in my nostrils.

At one point, not long before I was due to leave school, my dad was keen for me to go into the force. He even got me the forms to go to Hendon. However, one of the best decisions ever made, by me, or policing in general, was for me to go into acting. I think that's such an important thing for parents to do, though I understand it can be difficult now I'm a parent: to give them the space to be themselves. Completely understandably, Dad saw it as an alien industry with very little security, compared to the familiar world of policing.

Though I genuinely think there must be a copper gene. It's been quite dangerous over the years, especially in the US. I've had to work hard to prove to some people that I wasn't a cop. I look exactly like one. And I think I have that instinct to ask questions that coppers have, not because I want to arrest them but because I genuinely want to know more about them. When I'm interviewing someone, I often have a sense when they're not telling the truth and I'll use my dad's technique of leaving a silence, which most people immediately rush to fill with words, flattered that you're showing a genuine interest.

---

* Hint: you hurt your ribs.

17

As an actor, I've played police officers a few times over the years. The first job I got out of drama school was at the Westcliff Palace Theatre in a play called *Staircase*, directed by Richard Wilson, starring John Thaw and Charles Dyer, who had written the play.* It was about an ageing gay couple who own a barbershop in the East End of London and was effectively a two-hander with John and Charles playing the couple (though it was clear to all of us that Richard should have played the part).†

I was the assistant stage manager, which meant making sure the props were all set out before the performance, and I had a small part that basically involved me as the voice of a policeman delivering a summons, and I think at one point I had to play the upstairs lodger's legs.

It's a story of two men who were living when homosexuality is a crime. And at one point, one of them is charged with soliciting and receives a summons. So I'm dressed as a policeman, though you can only see my silhouette. And I knock on the door to deliver the summons to John's character.

One night, John and I were having dinner before the show and I mentioned that it was my birthday and that my mum and dad were coming in, and John just smiled and said, 'How lovely.' So that night, it comes to my line in the show and I knock on the door and go to say my line and John says, 'Yes, officer?' but this time, he stands to the side, so the audience can see me, including, in the front row, my mum and dad. And I do my line and John has his back to the audience and is absolutely twinkling, grinning at me the whole time. I'll never

---

* I still the remember the feeling of picking up my first ever cheque as an actor. £100. Get in.

† Even now 'I don't believe it'. Sorry.

forget that. He's in the middle of a two-hander that lasts for almost three hours, with so many lines and so much weight on him, but he was generous enough to let a very young and inexperienced actor have his moment. He didn't have to do that. But he did, because that was the size of the man. He was a hero to me before I met him but my admiration for him only grew working with him. Both him and Richard were both tremendously kind and generous to me.

John bought me a bottle of Moët & Chandon and it was the first champagne I had ever tasted, when I drank it a few months later with my mum after getting my first part on television.

A few years after leaving drama school, I was playing a copper again in an episode of *Birds of a Feather*. I mainly remember because they had to shoot me exclusively from the left-hand side. My girlfriend at the time and I had come back from me playing (extremely bad) village cricket to find someone relieving themselves against the wall of the small cottage where we were living. She quite reasonably asked him to stop pissing against our house, only to be told to F off. I'd gone to have a little chat with him and after some raised voices he'd apologised, held his hand out to shake mine and, when I grasped it, cracked me with a, to be fair to him, pretty solid left hook. After a bit more of a scuffle, where I ended up on top of him, efficiently punching the tarmac either side of his head, before landing one solid right, we were dragged apart and went our separate ways. But the next morning I had scabbed knuckles, and a fully closed and impressively purple and yellow right eye, which even extended television make-up couldn't quite hide. The legendary director Tony Dow, who had directed *Only Fools and Horses*, was very kind to me and let me do the whole scene filming me from the side. For the next few years my retina would continue to bleed.

After I'd left *Eastenders* I was playing a detective in a series called *Without Motive*. We shot in the morgue at Kingston upon Thames. Jane Hazlegrove, who is a lovely woman and a great actress, was brave enough to lie on the drain table where they carried out real autopsies for most of the day with only a sheet over her. As soon as I entered the morgue there was that smell that I hadn't smelled for more than thirty years and it suddenly took me back to being a little boy again, running to hug my dad's legs and smelling it on him when I pressed my face against his trousers. I hadn't thought about it for thirty years, though would do every time I set foot in one of the many morgues I've been in since, but, in that way that smells can, I was transported right back there, a little boy, excited my dad was home, and I realised it was that smell on my dad's trousers. It was the smell of formaldehyde.

Beach Fire

'Do you know there's a rumour they put formaldehyde in the beer in these parts to preserve it, Ross?'

I'm forty-two years old, on a beach in East Timor, wondering why Tom* has waited for me to drink four beers before he tells me this interesting fact. Still, as I swill it around my mouth, I reckon it's cold and it's fizzy and it's the last day of filming on a hell of a trip, so we order another round.

East Timor is an island in between Australia, Indonesia and Papua New Guinea and in 2006 was an extremely volatile place to be. It was at that point the youngest democracy in the world and saying there were growing pains would be putting it mildly. There were violent uprisings every couple of days and the streets were full of UN and foreign army vehicles. We were there making an episode of *Gangs*, as it was estimated that two thirds of the youth of East Timor were involved in some sort of gang and they were starting to gain political power. We'd spent days driving through neighbourhoods of burned-out buildings covered in gang graffiti and camps set up to house those burned out of their homes, with the constant hum of violence in the air. There were bullet holes in the window frames of our hotel. We'd just finished a long day interviewing various figures in the

---

* Tom Watson, thank you for everything you did on every show we worked on together (which was a lot!).

gangs, who fought each other with crude home-made bows and arrows and slings to gain power. I interviewed one guy with a twelve-inch nail still poking out of his head. It all felt depressingly intractable, as the poverty and high unemployment drove people into gangs, which drove the violence and made East Timor such a dangerous country at the time and not the sort of place likely to attract foreign investment. We'd already been in East Timor for two weeks without doing anything, after a muck-up with the wrong sort of tapes for our camera meant we had to wait for someone to bring new tapes from London for us to even begin filming. I'd started every morning with a run and then a relaxing swim, only to be greeted after two weeks in by Mauricio, our fixer,* running toward me waving his arms and shouting, 'Ross, Ross, why are you swimming on snake beach?!'

But now we've finished filming and Mauricio has found us a shack on the beach. They split open a massive fish and grilled it over an open fire. For the first time since we'd been there, our muscles unclenched a little. We were sitting on a tropical beach, around the bay from Dili, the capital city where we're staying, eating fish just pulled out of the water, and drinking beers as the sun sets behind the palm trees.

'Cheers, Mauricio,' muttered Tom. Actually, where was Mauricio? There's no mobile phone service and nobody seemed to know where he was. We half-heartedly called his name out for a bit, in case he was nearby, but then they brought more

---

* A fixer is a local journalist, or knowledgeable expert who you hire to help you get access to tell the story you need to tell. They are an absolutely essential part of the team, often working at great personal risk and we would quite literally be nowhere without them. People seem to think we're out there with teams of bodyguards or security, but they draw unwarranted attention so we rely on local knowledge. So it's usually just us and the fixers.

beers. A little while later, a Suzuki open-top jeep zooms right up to us and it's Mauricio.

'We must go,' he says. 'Now.'

'Mate, we're not going anywhere. Have some fish, have a beer.' I was on my sixth by this point and was quite up for staying on that beach until the sun came up again. Mauricio shook his head frantically. 'You have to go now, look across the bay, look across the bay,' he said, pointing. The sky was a vibrant orange and pink, streaked with clouds but in the distance, around the bay in the distance, I could see the orange glow of flame and smoke rising.

'What's that?' I asked.

'That's your hotel,' said Mauricio.

We started moving then. On the way Mauricio explained that today's uprising had hit upon the plan of stealing land by burning down the land registry office so there could be a land grab. And the land registry office just happened to be next door to our hotel. Luckily our hotel was safe but that couldn't be said for the land registry office; an Australian guy was standing on a ladder forlornly tipping a single bucket of water onto the flames. Gas canisters were starting to explode. That night, parts of Dilli were on fire and the smell of burning hung in the air.

The next morning I woke up with a shocker of a hangover. When I saw Tom at breakfast, he was looking similarly grey-green. Whether it was the formaldehyde in the beer or smoke inhalation, it was hard to pinpoint.

'This is the worst hangover I've ever had,' he croaked.

An Argument with Johnnie

'This is the worst hangover I've ever had,' I croaked. Next to my bed in a hotel room in Venezuela is an empty bottle of Johnnie Walker red. Never a good sign number one. I stumble to the bathroom and look in the mirror. As I grimace weakly to myself, I see I have knocked out most of my top front teeth.* Again. Never a good sign number two.

I am forty-seven years old, obscenely hungover and I need to access emergency dentistry in Venezuela.

My love/hate relationship with Johnnie Walker had begun eight years previously in Brazil, while I was making a film for *Gangs*.† It was the first *Gangs* we ever made, after I'd come back from a trip to the US to make a documentary about guns in the US and ended up successfully pitching the idea of a series of documentaries about different gangs around the world to Sky. The favelas around Rio have been the location for violently fought drugs wars for years and we were there to

---

* This is not quite as scary as it sounds. After many years playing rugby, there's not much of the actual original front teeth left anyway. But the fake enamel looked like broken windows.

† Though, to be honest, it still has nothing on my hate/hate relationship with Cinzano, which began with me drinking a bottle of it at an Essex house party when I was sixteen and ended with me retching into a concrete plant pot on the way home from the party. The flower pot is still there and I still can't go near the stuff.

24

meet members of one of the biggest gangs, Comando Vermelho or Red Command.

We flew in over a favela called Rocinha and I learned how the favelas grew up in and around the city as Brazilians fled poverty in the countryside and landed there. It was only when you were there you saw how intertwined with the city they were. From the sun lounger of my very nice hotel, I could see two hardcore favelas to one side and two to the other. At night, I would watch children kicking footballs, training with the youth coaches at Flamengo on the beach when it was cool enough to practise. We met gang members, watched people buying and selling drugs. The thick smell of sewage and barbecuing meat hung in the air. Precarious shacks crowded on top of each other. At one point, we were due to meet some gang members on the roof of a house and were just wondering where they were when they suddenly appeared, jumping across the roofs. Ecstasy had recently arrived in Rio and people were openly off their faces on it in the streets. A few years later, I would return to Rio when the drug of choice was cracky cracky (crack cocaine) and a toilet freshener that increased people's sex drive. I would walk down and watch barely pubescent pregnant girls take punters into rooms made of cardboard boxes to have sex with them. But back then it was all new to me. And I was very much out of my comfort zone.

Especially the prison we went to. Brazil's prison population was 250,000 (about the same size as Southampton). I went in alongside an evangelical group doing a prison visit. The preacher in a suit implored them to turn their backs on gangs and find Jesus, and they screamed and raised their arms to the sky. I saw young men crying uncontrollably at the hymns, undone by the thought of redemption – and I could see why. The prison was a converted office space. There were bottles jammed into the bars, full of urine, and plastic bags full of faeces. It was extremely hot and very humid and loud with constant shouting. Hundreds of people packed into these tiny cells, hardly enough room for them to stand upright. There were ropes strung between cells to carry parcels and messages. There were no windows. The air was still and smelled of thousands of bodies crushed together. Sweat poured down your face and down from the ceiling. We were told not to look up because if the liquid got in your eye it would cause an infection. I had heard the term hellhole before but never fully understood it till then.*

I would go back to my room at the end of long, hard days and I'd crack open the Johnnie Walker miniatures and have them with bottles of Coke in my minibar. When it was time to check out, I went through my bill and I realised they hadn't charged me for the four whiskies. I didn't want to get anyone in trouble, so I went to the guy on reception and said, 'Here, take my credit card and charge me for the miniatures of whisky.' But he wouldn't take it. My Portuguese was essentially non-existent, and his English wasn't great, so I kept trying to give him my card and he kept saying, no. Finally, I convinced him to take it away with him and to take the money for the whisky (remember this is four miniatures). I was absolutely sure he would get in trouble if his bosses found out he hadn't charged for something, so I felt like I'd done a small, good thing.

I get to the airport, get on the plane out of Rio and it goes via São Paulo to refuel and take on more passengers. We're waiting on the runway. So I turn on my mobile phone.

---

* Only a few years before, I would have been horrified to turn up on an acting job if the breakfast had run out, or the coffee wasn't hot enough.

This was back in the days when they were bricks with an extendable aerial. And it rings and someone says, 'Hello, Mr Kemp? This is Barclays. Have you just bought twenty thousand pounds' worth of phone cards in Rio?' In Rio at that point, phone cards were effectively a currency. You could buy food and petrol with them. I've never said anything as quickly as I said, 'Kill the card!'

Eight years later, I'm in Venezuela. And I've had to go and ask our fixer to try and help me find an emergency dentist. As I spoke to my team, I gradually pieced together what had happened. After a gruelling last day of a gruelling schedule of filming I had gone back to the hotel bar and drunk a bottle of Johnnie Walker. I was told afterwards that people were staying clear of me and calling me Senor Loco. And at some point, I tripped or slipped and slammed face down against the marble bartop. Now, my mouth was a mixture of various types of dental work and it didn't take very much but I lost a fair percentage of what was there. What I should have done at that point was go back to my room and make preparations for an emergency dentist. Not order another bottle of whisky. People told me that I was spitting bits of tooth out in between sips. Paramedics were called but when they arrived Senor Loco didn't want to leave his friend Johnnie. So understandably they left.

Venezuela would not be near the top of my list of places to find a dentist. In spite of the fact that Venezuela had more oil than any other country on the planet, its economy was in pieces. Chavez came to power on a ticket of removing corruption, repairing the infrastructure of the country and helping the poor. But it was on the point of collapse when we arrived. Crime had spun out of control and there had been 17,000 murders in a population of just under 30 million.

People were kidnapped for ransom frequently. We went to Caracas: 3 million people, many of whom live in the barrios or slums. We followed policemen on patrol with the constant threat of violence. There were 18,000 gangs and many of them specialised in kidnapping. It was estimated there were three kidnappings a day. The corruption was off the scale, with police rumoured to be involved in a substantial proportion of crime in the country. I was told that the police were effectively just another criminal gang. I saw children carried into hospital, shot, their families wailing. Crime and violence had become a way of life. The zebra crossing at the back of our hotel was known locally as the cashpoint, as people on mopeds would just crash into anyone crossing it and rob them as they lay on the floor.

Like eight years previously in Brazil, we'd gone to a prison here as well. If anything, this one was even more memorable. This prison had light and air. Shops and barbers. The prisoner who ran it, Leo, wore a bright white T-shirt and told me that people were treated better in prison than in the outside world. There were no guards, Leo and his companions ran it. The authorities took people in and out, but while they were there it was Leo in charge. There was a basketball court and visiting teams from other gangs would come to play games in front of a crowd. Leo was very charismatic, surrounded by bodyguards with expensive Austrian guns. He had a satellite dish. If you stayed on the right side of Leo, were useful to him, you could stay in the good bit of the prison with the good drugs, the nice food, the tattooist, the dentist and the women who regularly visited. But if you did something wrong, or weren't any use to him, then you had to go to the other side.

In the other side, it was something else. The smell of rotting sewage and chemical tang of crack. Half-dead skeletal prisoners, many of them ill, huge numbers of them with glaucoma. At one point, I looked above me in one of the rooms and there were hammocks strung across the ceiling and I asked what they were for and was told that they only came to collect the dead once a week. In another room there was, of all things, a massive display of an inflatable snowman covered in Christmas lights. At this point the country was suffering from regular blackouts, but in prison they had a Christmas light show. It was incredibly intense and emotionally exhausting. Hence the whisky. Hence our fixer finding me an emergency dentist.

The next morning I spent hours with a bottle-and-half-of-whisky hangover, while a very angry Venezuelan dentist, who clearly assumed I was a spy and had been sent there by the US to undermine their socialist utopia, glared at me. She had been woken up on her one day off per week to be greeted by a man who smelled like a distillery. As I sat in the chair, she picked up a stainless-steel chisel and a hammer. She leaned in between my legs, smiled at me, then pushed her knee against my chest and swung the hammer back. For more than ten minutes she went at it, every swing a protest against US imperialism. Jarring up into my head, bouncing around my hangover-addled skull. At one point, she put down the hammer only to hold up a particularly industrial bit of equipment, I asked her if there was a chance of any anaesthetic and she just laughed.

As she knelt on my chest and brandished an even bigger metal implement, I tried to splutter out that I was making a documentary. But there was no way she believed me.

Little Moments

Sometimes all you need is for someone to believe in you. School started to change for me when I went to secondary school. Most lessons were still a bit of a slog. But I was getting properly into my rugby and now school plays and I had also found a teacher there who believed in me. And told me so. Mr Golledge. He taught art. He had long grey hair, a beard and glasses. He looked like a druid in a suit. But by God he had a voice on him. He was such an interesting blend of things. One of those intense sergeant majors of a teacher who the tough kids are genuinely scared of but also very much respect. But he was also a bit of a hippy. I remember he was always a fan of the kids who did art that came from somewhere inside them. Some kids would draw these very neat drawings and he would pass them by. But the messy picture that expressed something inside them, he'd stop there and compliment it. I still remember one painting I did of a feather that he told me was the best in the class. You carry those things with you, when you're used to teachers focusing on the things you can't do as well.*

Mr Golledge was into photography and so I got into it. My parents bought me a Ricoh 35 mm camera for Christmas. He

_____

* Along with Mr Golledge, there was Mr Gibbons, a huge red-haired man with mutton chops, but he mainly liked me because he was the rugby coach and I was in the county team.

taught me to use a dark room and develop and print my own pictures. I remember being especially proud of a photograph I took of a plant in the woods round the back of our house – a blade of grass with seeds frozen to it.

I got into looking at these old photography magazines he had in massive stacks. And it wasn't long after Vietnam. That era of incredible war photographs. I remember this fascination, going through them. I remember one *Sunday Times* magazine which had war pictures of Vietnam and it also had these adverts for whisky and cigars. It was this mixture of astonishing photographs but also the idea of this grown-up, cosmopolitan world (I still have it, so apologies, Mr Golledge).

One day, in WHSmiths, I saw a book with *WAR* in black letters on a red background. It was a history of war photography, from the first time war photographs had been taken during the Crimean War, right the way through to photographs taken of the Troubles in Northern Ireland. Some of them were utterly brutal: Pacific beaches covered with bodies. I didn't know it then but I'm sure the idea of capturing these images in these extreme environments, of telling these stories, I'm sure that was a seed that was planted then. It brought together so many things at the same time.

Mr Golledge encouraged me to act too, told me that I had talent. It had started with the games we'd all played and the Dracula plays and moved on to impressions of teachers. I realised I could do something that not everyone could do, or even wanted to do, but that maybe I wanted to do it a bit more seriously.

So my mum got me this drama teacher called Mrs Feakins, who I'd met when I was at junior school and she wrote a play for us. I was playing an old guy and I had to have a walking stick. She told me I needed to stop waving it around and use it to actually walk with. If my character had a walking stick, that was because they needed one to walk. And that was the first time I'd thought about that. Up until that point, I'd liked getting the laughs and getting the applause and the attention. But that idea of a character, of capturing every aspect of them, I was just fascinated by it. My mum paid for private lessons with Mrs Feakins once a week. She freed me up, at a time when academically I still didn't feel very confident. In that hour, I developed an appetite for taking drama seriously. Dot Feakins also knew about mime, so she taught me about that and then suggested I go for the LAMDA exams. And in the first test I got a 90. I'd never got a 90 in anything in my life. The next time, the examiner said, 'I can't give 101 but I'll give you 100.'

In the end it was wanting to be in plays that encouraged me to read. Because I knew I'd have to read if I wanted to act. We put on a school play called *Hijack over Hygienia*, where I played a kind of jester figure and I realised that I was able to read and learn lines. So that broke the back of it for me. Later in my life, people would seem to think that being a 'luvvie' was some sort of disqualification from things. From politics or making documentary films. But I never saw acting as separate from real life. There would be these moments in the middle of acting where you could be dressed in a costume and you were saying lines that someone else had written, describing someone else's life, but there was something there that felt true. You could bring parts of yourself, like when you made a picture Mr Golledge liked that didn't look like the thing but still captured something true about it. I just fell in love with it. It was like I'd found my tribe.

Tribes

The more I've been around the world, the surer I've become that the key to it all is tribes. Humans naturally want to be part of some sort of meaningful grouping. For some people that's supporting Leyton Orient, for others it's line dancing. We want to feel part of something. Who am I and what do I stand for? The first thing you work out is who you're not. You see it all the time in politics as well, all around the world. What is the threat? Who should you be scared of? Who am I safer with? It's a lot easier to point at groups and say 'We're not them', than come up with who you are. It's just human nature. But it's serious stuff. And as I've travelled, it seems as if polarisation is only getting more extreme.

A classic example was the horrific violence between the Hutu and Tutsi tribes in Rwanda, who in so many ways have no significant cultural or linguistic differences. But whether you came from the farmer or herder tribe became the basis of a horrific genocide.

I've seen what happens all around when people try and draw other boundaries over pre-existing tribal identities. It's the cause of much human misery.

I've seen at first-hand the devastating violence that accompanies tribal conflict. I've seen the horrendous experiments in human nature that wars are close up. Human beings can quickly resort to very base things. If you and I are friends

33

and someone shoots you, it becomes personal. That becomes used by certain people to extend conflict over generations. People live with a constant need for revenge. I've been to places where people have forgotten the reason they originally started fighting but generations later they still are.

We tend to think about tribal violence as happening 'over there' but anyone who lived through the Troubles knows how close to home it can be. I think of me and the other boys growing up in Essex. The Abbott's Close Gang. I think of the gang members I've seen on every continent. What is a gang in essence but that urgent need to belong?

The reason I started to make documentaries is because of one gang member I interviewed called Bloodhound. It was as part of a documentary called *Lethal Attraction: Why Americans Love Guns*. It's a subject I've always been interested in. Possibly because of all that running around with imaginary guns as a child. We went to Compton in California, to interview members of the two most famous of its estimated 700 gangs: the Bloods and the Crips.* Bloodhound had a red bandana, dreadlocks tipped with red plastic balls, and a small teardrop tattooed under his eye. I could immediately tell he was fiercely intelligent. He was educated about history, especially the history of civil rights in the US. He was funny and charismatic but the range of choices he'd faced were startling. Telling me in an utterly matter-of-fact way what would happen if we went to the wrong area, or if he saw a Crip where they shouldn't

---

* I remember talking to two officers from the county sheriff's office, who were laden down with guns; they told me that back in the day, if you were a Blood, you would refuse to even use the letter C. You'd call Compton, 'Bompton'. If you were inviting your friend for a cup of coffee you'd say, 'Bup of boffee'. On one level it was utterly farcical, but so many people died over it.

34

be. He told me he'd been shot twenty-three times and when I raised an eyebrow at that, he pulled up his T-shirt to show me the map of scar tissue across his body, entry and exit wounds that he referred to as his 'stripes'. He'd been first shot when he was twelve years old, trying to sell weed through a car window. He'd leaned in to ask them, 'What would you like?' And they'd replied, 'I'll take your life.' One of the six shots hit a testicle, which he said had swollen to the size of a grapefruit. But he told me not to worry as he'd subsequently fathered three children. He'd been shot five times in the chest and, when he was on the ground, they shot him again. He took my finger and placed it under his chin to feel where the bullet had entered, poked out his tongue to show where it had taken the tip off and then finally pointed at the gap in his skull above his eyes where the bullet had been removed.

'Execution style,' he said, calmly, just the way it was. He showed me the hollow point bullet wounds in his side that had caused him to have a colostomy bag for a year.

He got out the Tec-9 machine pistol he carried around with him at all times, the AK-47 and pump action shotgun he kept for situations that 'required' it. I remember thinking that if he'd been born fifteen blocks away, maybe he'd have been a lawyer or a doctor, or a schoolteacher. It made me immediately think about what that gang (or brotherhood as he called it) meant to him, what it was giving him he wasn't getting from anywhere else in his life. A place to belong and a place to matter. You could tell he was scared and wanted to get out. But he couldn't. He was trapped. He wasn't dripping in gold, driving a low-rider. He had three kids and a blocked toilet. He was as far away from the MTV portrayal of gang culture as you could be. Beyond the simple narratives of bad people doing bad things, this felt like a subject that needed to be explored.

I dread to think how much of my life I have spent waiting around for members of a gang to turn up. It sounds obvious, but members of a gang often have quite a lot going on (when they're not asleep). They're often quite distractable. There's a lot of things that can get in the way of a gang member making their appointment with you. Plus, we're never paying them, so the only real leverage is if they want to get some point of view out there and tell their stories. There are plenty of gangs where that's the case. The intersection of crime, drugs, and politics is especially tangled all around the world. You have gangs that form for a specific reason, then end up becoming a criminal gang. You have gangs who use the proceeds of the drug trade to fund their political activities. You also have political opponents to the government who are labelled gangs to discredit them and justify violence against them.

But for street gangs, there's no real agenda. So often you're relying on them wanting to be recorded. So there's a lot of 'we hate them because they killed my friend, so I'm going to kill one of them' type interviews on the cutting room floor.

Eight years after I met Bloodhound, I met up with some New Orleans gang members among the ruins of houses devastated by Hurricane Katrina. They wore red scarves over their faces and were covered in tattoos. One of them told me the cross on his forehead meant that he was a killer. He said in his husky voice, 'It wasn't for decoration.' They told me how they swam in the 'dirty-ass water' of Hurricane Katrina. They blamed the violence on the lack of job opportunities. If no one was giving them anything, they felt they had to take it. With their trousers low around their waists and their fingers on the triggers of their guns, they told me that they 'took what they wanted'. One told me he was a 'three-time loser' and he would hold court with police on the street if they turned up because he knew next time he would be locked up forever.

One described how his pistol 'made his dick hard'. How getting a gun was as easy as 'getting a cold drink'. They were young men, boys who believed that the police, the courts, the government were dirty and not for people like them. They described where they were as 'hell'. It was hard to get past the bravado. But it's what I've always been so drawn to . . . What was this hardness masking? They were angry because they felt abandoned, because they had nothing. Nothing but the thought that they were in control of their lives when they were the ones pointing a gun at someone else.

When you're involved in gangs there are strict rules and demands. If you come from a background where there's not much structure, that can feel enticing. There are all sorts of reasons an individual joins a gang. That often includes fear. In El Salvador, if you're invited to join a gang and say 'no', you won't live long, or your family won't. There is no choice. But there are kids on the streets of Britain who are stabbing each other over gang loyalty. This isn't just happening over there, away from us. It's happening in my own country.

Every day in the UK, three people between the age of ten and nineteen are being admitted to hospital with stab wounds. What we need to do is give kids options. You've got to look at what causes a young person to carry a knife. When you speak to young people, it's almost always defensive, it comes from a place of fear. But you're twice as likely to be stabbed if you're carrying a knife. They ask you to show them better options. They feel let down by the police, by the government. These are young people who treat life as a war. They refer to 'the enemy' and 'civilians'. The more we can try and understand these problems in all their complexity, the more we might be able to come up with solutions. Because things only change when people know there's a problem and decide it matters to them. Politicians won't do anything about an issue that doesn't win votes. You can't vote for a party who have a policy on an issue if you don't know that issue exists. I still believe that an unbiased media has a role in informing the populace so they can decide what matters to them.

I met one guy who was an associate of the Mexican mafia in LA. He had tattoos of the people he had killed on his shaved head. When I met him, he had a dent in his head from being attacked from behind with a long barbell in prison. Hence the tattoo on his forehead that read 'I'm still standing'. But while he was inside, he had received a message. Messages are sent across from prison to prison, passed internally in any number of prisoners, as they're moved between prisons, in a process known as 'keistering'.* For understandable reasons, micro-writing is a prized skill.† You have to be able to write the lord's prayer five times on a bit of paper the size of a thumbnail. And one day, a message comes out of someone's backside that brings the news that the man from the Mexican mafia has got to take care of something for his organisation. He needs to 'get rid of' Juan. The only problem is, there's

---

* That's an episode of *Postman Pat* you *really* don't want to watch.
† I made a documentary in a UK prison, where I went in and experienced some of what a prisoner does. At one point, you get undressed and sit on a machine that is designed to detect any objects you may have hidden *inside* yourself, which is called 'banking' and is a massive source of drugs, weapons and contraband in prison. But it doesn't find all of them. The record haul is seven mobile phones. They once found a prisoner trying to bank a 9-inch kitchen knife into the prison. Never mind punishment, that person should have some sort of stage show. They must have a colon like Mary Poppins' carpet bag.

no surname in the message. And there are two Juans. So which Juan should he get rid of? This Juan? Or that Juan? He decides the only way to be sure is to get rid of both. That's the kind of life he lived.

We were out with him one evening, getting some food, when he spotted a rival gang member. As a sign of respect, you have to say your name and where you're from. So there are these two Latino gangs, all carrying guns, apart from me. And they line up in the carpark outside a store and everyone moves down the line saying their name and where they're from, like the most terrifying breaking-the-ice session ever. I know that if this goes wrong and someone feels disrespected, they might start shooting.

'Lil Man, Northside.'

And she says, 'Slick, Northside Riva.'

'Baby Face, Southside.'

And then they get to me. 'Ross Kemp, Battersea. Parkside.'

How Not to Be a Boyfriend

Her dad didn't like me. It was made clear that I was a bit rough, from the wrong side of the tracks. Literally. Where we lived, the divide between the fancy and less fancy bit of town was the railway through the middle.

But more than that, I was in sixth-form college, retaking my O-levels before I went to study drama at Southend Tech. She was studying to go to university.

Where they lived, the houses were larger and detached and the neighbours all seemed to be competing to see who had the biggest pot of geraniums. He was inordinately proud of their new porch. He had a beard and a big moustache, and pomaded hair in a side parting, and an upright, quite old-fashioned bearing. He'd done well for himself. When I got to their house, his wife would be playing classical music on their piano. I was used to my mum and dad dancing to rock and roll on in the back room, so it was a very different mood.

He had older sons who had been to Oxbridge and then he had his daughter, the light of his life. Here I was, this mop-haired son of a copper and a hairdresser, who apparently wanted to be an actor of all things. But I loved her, it was first love – if you put aside the girls I'd done my Dracula plays with.

The previous summer, I'd worked in his building supplies shop, at first in the office doing filing but when they realised how rubbish I was at that, I ended up in the back moving heavy things about, which suited me fine. Except for the fact that some of the blokes who worked there tried to come up with ever more ingenious ways to get me the sack. After a bit of classic 'tartan paint and long weight' style teasing, they decided it would be fun to tell me that it was a tradition for everyone to take it in turns to take a rest in the back. So I get myself comfortable. Two minutes later and the boss comes through and gives me the sack for sleeping on the job. It was a good reminder to me: always play your own game, not someone else's.

That summer, I had taken to wearing my Essex County rugby shorts and often I would also go commando. I don't know why. Perhaps I thought I'd cracked the secret to never having to buy underpants. One day that summer, her dad took me aside and whispered to me, 'If I ever see you round here again, flashing your testicles, I'm going to cut them off.'* Not only did I believe him from the tone of voice, but I knew he had access to some very serious cutting equipment too.

There had been some sort of falling out between me and her. I think she'd gone away for a trip abroad and we'd split up, or maybe I thought we were going to because of the energetic way she described her German pen pal. There was some sort of drama. But I had resolved to fix this by going round to her house, welcoming her back home and giving her a big bouquet of flowers. It had taken me a week of shifts waiting tables at the golf club to pay for this gigantic display of floral affection.

So I made sure I was wearing underwear and off I went, all dressed up, doused in my dad's Brut, ready to win her back and salvage my reputation with her family.

---

*   Fair enough.

I had been driving my mum's riverweed-green Vauxhall Viva up until a few months before, but someone had swerved across the road and crashed into it while it had been parked around the corner from my girlfriend's house. Even though they'd caught the bloke who'd done it, it still felt like this was a mark against me. The fact that this was one of the few times I hadn't actually been behaving like a boy racer made it even worse.

However it also meant that I was driving my dad's GS Citroën Club. A not very impressive car but one that could definitely motor. And, of course, Citroën being a French company, they didn't put the hand brake down where it normally is. It was up on the dashboard, on a kind of pole with a trigger and it was a slightly fiddly mechanism involving multiple stages to engage the brake.

It was one of those beautiful warm early September evenings. I've learned my lesson, so I park at the top of their drive, so no one can crash into it, and then I saunter down their long drive feeling good. I've checked myself in the mirror, I'm looking sharp, I'm feeling sharp. I have highlights in my quiff.

I ring the doorbell. Her dad answers the door and I see him clock me and he's not delighted but he's also not horrified. But then, within a split second, I see him look over my shoulder with a look of genuine horror. And before I can turn to see what he's looking at, I get propelled forwards, lifted up into the air and into his arms by my dad's GS Citroën Club, which has built up quite a bit of momentum as it followed me slowly down the long drive. It smashes the pots of geraniums, puts a crack in the windows of the new porch and I'm later informed terrified his wife and daughter, who when the whole house shook thought there had been some sort of explosion or earthquake. He shoves me off him and I'm left standing there, not quite sure what to do, but still holding up my bouquet of flowers. All I could think of was to say, 'These are for your daughter.'

And all he could say, with a high, anguished voice was, 'What have you done to my house?'

Things fizzled out with her, pretty much there and then.

I was absolutely in love with her. My heart was broken, as were my finances by the time I'd paid for the repairs to his porch. I ended up serving a lot of prawn cocktails and Blue Nun at the golf club to pay for that. I'd never understood what people meant when they said they were lovesick, but after that I took to my bed for three days. It didn't take long before she had found someone who was much more suitable. He probably wore pants and everything.

If the equivalent of seventeen-year-old me ever turns up at my door, seeking to spend time with one of my daughters, I'll definitely encourage him not to flash his testicles.

How Not to Go on Holiday

You never want to finish a holiday with extremely sore testicles and people pointing at you and whispering 'that's him' as you pass.

It's the mid-nineties and I've been on holiday with my girlfriend at the time in the Bermuda Triangle, where strange things famously happen and go missing. We don't know each other that well yet. There are hundreds of keys there, which are tiny sand-covered islands that have formed on coral reefs. Our hotel is full of pilots who had just popped there for the day, for some reason. It's also slap bang in the middle of a major route for transporting drugs into the US.

There's a bar on the main island we're staying on that has a speciality called a Goombay Smash, which is a cocktail made with pineapple juice and two types of rum and gin. And, though I've not been able to find this in the official recipes, I'm pretty certain this particular version had something 'herbal' in it. They said you were only meant to have one, but I decided this meant that, me being me, I could have at least three. Two hours later, I'm riding the golf buggy, trying to find a secluded beach to have a nice lie-down, and I'm absolutely certain that we're being followed. I keep saying, 'Look, there behind us. Someone's following us.' And my girlfriend is turning around but she can't see anyone. Eventually we realise that what I'm seeing is the rod that holds up the roof of the golf buggy. I'm a Goombay Smashed dog chasing his own tail.

Eventually we find a beach. After a little while, the effects of the Goombay Smash have receded enough for us to enjoy the beach. But I decide I need to drive us to the fresh golden sand I can see in the distance. However, it turns out that when the tide comes in, that sand gets very soft. After two hours of trying to dig the buggy out of the beach, we give up and walk two hours back to the hotel, plastered in sand.

The next day we decide to take a boat out. At that point, I didn't have much experience with boats. The boat man in the harbour says that whatever we do, we don't want to moor too close to the beach. Because when the tide goes out your boat will be left high and dry. And the tide won't come back in for six hours. He also tells us that an Italian couple who had made that mistake had failed to make a fire, or stay close for warmth and had died of exposure.

I'm nodding and reassuring him that this won't happen. And we take this thirty-foot speedboat over to this other key we've heard about.

One thing is for certain, neither of us should be in charge of it. We cruise around for a bit and pass lots of islands, until we see the most idyllic (they are all stunning, to be fair).

And we moor up. My girlfriend asks if I'm certain that's far enough from shore and I say I'm 100 per cent sure it is. And we've brought a picnic with us and a bottle of rum and our ice and we have the entire island to ourselves. So we fall asleep under the shade of a coconut tree and life feels extremely good. But, as the sun starts to go down, it starts to get a bit cold. All we're wearing is swimming costumes and a T-shirt.

The prow of the boat is facing the island and the stern is facing the open sea. And I've taken up the propellor, which I

45

now try and put down. But it won't drop and that's when I realise that the boat is now sitting up on sand.

I persuade my girlfriend to put a snorkel on and go and dig out the front of the boat (what can I say, I'm a romantic). And I'm trying to push several tons of boat out. And as I'm watching, the tide is rushing out, like water out of a bath. So there we are, she's digging with bare hands, and I'm trying to push the boat but the top of the fibreglass is all cracked and I slip and cut the palm of my hand. And I'm getting wound up at the boat and calling it names, but really, of course, I'm wound up at myself. And this is serious because we know people have literally died after making the same mistake. We haven't told anyone exactly where we were going and there are about 1700 islands in the archipelago. The chances of them finding us feel pretty remote.

And my girlfriend just keeps saying, 'There must be a radio' and 'We need to look for the radio'. But I look everywhere, and I can't find one. I'm pulling open the cupboards and I'm cursing the good name of the people that have sent us off without a radio. So I decide, partly out of wounded pride, that I have to fix this situation with my manliness. Thinking of the Italian couple who died of exposure, I decide I'm going to need to build a fire to save us. It's not quite dark yet, but it will be very soon. So I go wandering off into the jungle and there's all these big land crabs who are scuttling under my feet and it looks as if the whole floor is moving. I dig this nice hole in the sand on the beach and I pull all this dry brush and these palm leaves out to it and I get this fire going nicely. But the leaves are burning too quickly, I realise I need something bigger to keep the fire alight for longer. So off I go, over the land crabs, deeper into the forest and there are these old disused wooden chairs and a little wooden table. And I do

46

think to myself 'That's odd', but this is life and death. I need to build a fire and I need to keep us alive and this is all my fault. I've got locked into this mindset that the only way this can be fixed is if I make this massive fire even more massive to keep us alive. I'm sweating, covered in sand, again. This is the second vehicle I've buried in less than twenty-four hours. This definitely isn't the impression I wanted to make on my new girlfriend.

So I'm dragging wood to the fire. Man must make fire. Woman not find radio on boat.

But she ignores me. So I get the chairs and the table back to the fire and I smash them up and they go on. And I'm finding anything made of wood and I'm smashing it and burning it. It's almost completely dark by this time, so by the light of my Bic lighter I find this enormous log and I go to lift it up and am surprised by how light it is. And I wedge it between these rocks and I give it a serious downward heel karate kick to break it in half so I can carry it back and burn it. And as soon as I did, this black tar poured out of the log, ran up my leg into my shorts and began to burn me. Or rather that's when all the ants that had been living inside the log, quite happily chewing on the wood, decide to defend themselves against this thing that's attacking them and run up my leg, biting as they go. They're pouring up my leg and into my shorts. And they're everywhere, literally everywhere, nipping and nipping. And I'm screaming and I come running out of the jungle, past my girlfriend and I dive into the ocean. I'm shrieking and they're coming off me and floating to the surface like an oil slick of ants. And that's when I hear a crackle of static.

And my girlfriend says: 'Mayday, mayday, we're stranded. Over.'

And that's when I realise she's found the radio. And it crackles immediately in reply: 'Are you the bastards that have set fire to our holy island? Over.'

And she looks down at me, whimpering, floating in the sea and behind us is a fire big enough to be seen from the moon. 'My boyfriend did, yes. Over.'

I spent the remaining days of that trip nursing my testicles and my pride. Not for the first or last time.

How Not to Go Swimming

I managed not to flash my testicles at my current father-in-law for a good few years. To be fair, I wasn't actually sure I had even flashed him. And even if I had, there was a good chance he wouldn't remember. I certainly couldn't remember anything.

I was woken to a bright Australian morning by my wife, Renée, nudging me firmly in the side. 'Ross, the police are downstairs,' she whispered.

Now this is never a good thing to wake up to. But certainly not when you're stark naked, with a world-ending hangover in the ludicrously strong Australian sunlight.

I groan. I am forty-nine years old and out in Australia where we'd been making a film about the Rebels and Hells Angels biker gangs, and when I'd finished filming, we took a trip to see my wife's family in Queensland. You're not allowed to swim in the sea in Queensland at certain times of the year because the crocs are spawning. When we go out there, we tend to all rent a house by the coast and make a family holiday of it. And where we are, the mangroves have been converted into land for houses. So you're very much on the crocs' territory. You get these fifteen-foot salties who are either horny or protective but either way extremely territorial. Queensland is also the home of the Irukandji jellyfish, a particularly small and venomous species. They look like an air bubble in the water but they can kill you.

49

The previous day, my father-in-law, who is known as Pug, and my brother-in-law, Dennis, and I decide to go out for a slap-up meal at an amazing restaurant on the beach we've been to before. Completely understandably there was a bit of 'who's this bloke?' when I first arrived on the scene. But now we get on brilliantly and I look forward to our nights out together. So, me in my lucky shorts and a T-shirt, we set off.*

Hours and hours later, we're still up. The place we're staying has this garden with coconut trees. We're sitting out drinking and laughing. The last thing I can remember is us in the garden in the early hours of the morning, agreeing that another bottle of red was a great idea.

And now the police are downstairs.

Did we go back into town? What the hell happened? I put some clothes on and my thongs and I go downstairs.†

There are two police officers. 'Are you Ross Kemp?' And at first I think maybe they recognise me off the television, so I nod. But they just go, 'Is *he* not Ross Kemp?', and I look outside where, crisping in the harsh morning sunlight is Pug, whose face is stuck to the table with red wine. And they're holding up my press ID card. 'Is this ID card yours, Ross Kemp?' They're holding a card with a picture of my face on it. I nod. They hold up my wallet. 'Is this wallet your wallet, Ross Kemp?' 'Are these shorts yours, Ross Kemp?' We go through the shorts, the underwear, me nodding yes to every

---

* My lucky shorts were given to me by an engineer in Sangin in Afghanistan to wear when I was cooling off in the river. The Taliban used to defecate upriver of Sangin. It was the location of some of the fiercest fighting in the entire conflict. It was an incredibly dangerous place. Those shorts have been around the world with me, so thank you, mate, for donating them.

† Australians call flip flops 'thongs', which always amuses me when I hear a big burly Australian bloke calling out, 'Has anyone seen my other thong?'

item of clothing. I can't work out if they're being obtuse or taking the micky.

'Now, Mr Kemp, I have to admit we assumed you'd been taken by a croc, when we were alerted to a pile of clothes and matched it up to reports of a bald man swimming in the sea in the early hours of the morning shouting, and I quote, "Come and have a go if you think you're hard enough."'

Now I'm pretty sure they've made that up but this detail does not go down well. So a little while later, Pug suggests we go and have breakfast at the same place we'd left the night before. By this time it's about 11 a.m. I've been told off by the police and multiple family members. Pug's reasoning is that once you're in the doghouse, you might as well make the most of it. So we walk down to the restaurant, go in and sit down, order breakfast. And there's this couple waving at us. And I wave back slightly confused.

'Hello mate. We're from New Zealand. We're the ones that found your stuff on the beach and gave them to the police. Glad you weren't eaten by a croc.'

I was so grateful to them, I bought them a bottle of sparkling wine. And then they bought us a bottle of sparkling wine. I look at Pug. 'Well it would be incredibly rude to send it back,' he says.

Eleven hours later, after dinner, we walk back home. 'Let's not go for a dip tonight,' I slur to Pug.

The Bends

One thing you really *really* don't want is to come up from a scuba dive and not be able to see the boat.

The Indian Ocean suddenly becomes an even bigger place. I glanced at my girlfriend at the time, who was spinning slowly in circles, trying to push herself up out of the water to see a bit further.

'Please tell me you see the boat, Ross,' she said.

I scanned all around us but couldn't see anything. No boat, no divers, no shore, just endless water. It was impossible to work out how far we'd drifted, and we had no way of calling for help. Oh dear.

I've always been obsessed with water. I learned to swim when I was very young; first, swimming lessons with my mum in the local pool, then the Norfolk coast, where the erosion and drift of sand had created these little natural pools deep enough that you can swim in them. And then, when I was older and could deal with the undertow, the sea in Wales. I loved the sensation of the waves. It's one of those central childhood memories, spending the whole day in the water. The kids there would take these planks of wood – this was before Boogie Boards came out – go out into the waves and ride them back to shore. Again and again. Your skin and your hair covered in salt and your mouth dry and having to be dragged out of the water because your lips were turning blue.

Some of the summers were chronic, of course. We nearly lost the caravan a couple of times when the wind came up and caught the awning like a spinnaker. But the summers I remember are those endless days with the sky that high bright blue.

You'd get up in the morning and catch mackerel, come home and slice them open. Put them straight on the barbecue. Then have them with salt and pepper and vinegar on bread. I've eaten a lot of things in different places around the world but there's very few breakfasts that come close to that.

I remember one year, looking out over the sea one day and I saw this family and they were going out in a rubber dinghy. They were all wearing wetsuits, heading out for a dive. And I remember thinking, 'I want to do that.'

I'd always been fascinated by the idea of being under the water. And especially of being able to breathe under it. When I would have a bath, as a kid, I'd get the squeezy bottle of washing up liquid in there, so I could make rocks and icebergs out of the bubbles and I'd have my scuba diving Action Man and I'd have him going down under the water and bringing ships up.* We'd be Thunderbird 4, rescuing someone deep under the sea. I was especially into the idea of shipwrecks.

So, pretty much as soon as I could afford it, in Cyprus one year on holiday, I got my PADI diving certification. The diving instructor was this Amazonian Swedish woman and my girlfriend at that time wasn't delighted that I spent seven hours a day of the holiday off with her.

Then the next year I wanted to go to the best place for diving and at that time that was the Maldives. At this point, in the mid-nineties, people were properly waking up to the

---

* Bubble bath?! Pure luxury.

fact that those amazing circular reefs, the atolls, weren't going to be there forever and we needed to make the most of them. So we went to this beachside diving resort for three weeks. The girlfriend I was with then had her diving certificate too. We're heading out first thing in the morning on these dhow boats, about thirty of us, diving every day. You'd get taken out to various dive sites and I'd buddy up with my girlfriend. The coral forms these amazing, complicated shapes like something from another planet, and just teeming with life. Thousands of brightly coloured fish, manta rays and sharks. Hundreds of black tip reef sharks. Something incredible to look at everywhere you looked. You'd spend a few hours diving, and then they'd take you back to the resort.

I got angry because loads of the tourists would go out and walk on the reefs. This delicate living thing and they'd go stomping across it picking up these crabs and sea urchins and these things we didn't know what they were but called squiddly diddlies, and they're putting them in buckets. Some of them were eating them but others were just leaving them outside their beach huts. So what I decided to do in the evening was to commando crawl up to the huts with a bucket of my own and put them all back in the sea. I did that every night we were there (luckily I never got caught).

On this particular morning, we get dropped off to dive these two submerged reefs. And there was a strong current between them. So we're down there and we get caught in this current and my girlfriend grabs hold of me and we're drifting along, looking below us, pointing at all the beauty, when I realise I can't see anyone else. I fin myself around in a circle and can't see anyone. So I signal that we should go up. This was in the days where you had a pretty basic rig. No fancy dive watches that tell you exactly how long you've been down, how much nitrogen there is in your system and plans your safety stops for you, flashing red if you're doing it wrong. You may have heard of the bends, which is the condition you can get if you come up from deep water too fast and the nitrogen in your bloodstream is released too quickly. It can make you pretty sick and in extreme cases even kill you. What this means is that if you go down past a certain point, you need to make safety stops, to give your body time to remove the nitrogen it has built up. This is all just to explain that if you're diving and you want to go back to the surface for any reason, say, for example you can't see any of the people you were diving with and you have no idea where they are and you want to get to the surface to see if you can spot them, you can't do it quickly if you've gone down past a certain point. So we did our five-minute safety stop at 5 metres and then we slowly went up to the surface.

'Ross, please tell me you can see the boat.' Oh dear.

Some people say it's the not knowing what's down there that scares them about deep water. I can tell you what's worse than not knowing. Knowing for an absolute certainty that there are hundreds of sharks.* To be fair, neither of us freaked out. But you definitely learn something about yourself in that scenario. We're there, floating on the surface, arm in arm, drifting slowly in the current. The day before, we'd gone diving and they'd chummed the water to attract the sharks. So we knew exactly how big they got. We agreed that there was no point trying to go in any one direction. We had no idea where we were so it made more sense to stay put. So we did. We

---

* To be clear, I am not bashing sharks. Sharks kill about ten people in an average year. People kill more than ten thousand sharks an hour. You are more likely to be killed by a pig or a vending machine than a shark.

were there for more than five hours, pretty much expecting something to come and take a bite out of us for the entire time. And I'm thinking that the sun is going to go down pretty soon. We're both dehydrated and my head looks like a bright red Rice Krispie by this point; a bald head burns and then it starts to bubble. Dry lips. Both of us burned to a crisp. At one point we heard engines and we're both calling out and I'm whistling as loudly as I can, both of us with these parched, dry throats. But it goes past us. That was hard. About half an hour later we heard engines again. And luckily, this time they hear us and come and drag us up into the boat. They're nothing to do with the resort, just out fishing. But they give us water and take us back. And when we get there, the dive masters are just sat by the beach. I'm so weak and sunburned, I try to grab one of them, but I can't. I chase them but can't catch them. Everything hurts from the sun. It turned out they'd never even noticed. Surely that's day one of divemaster school: don't forget any divers. Count them off and count them back in again.

I don't know what it says about me that that wasn't the only time I've been left in open water. The next time was a few years in a period of my life when I was suddenly spending time with people who were superyacht rich. Now, where I'd grown up, being richer meant you had a bigger garden, or telly, or an extra garage. Once I'd started on TV, at various points, I'd spent time with people who would be considered proper rich. Been to very nice houses, been in very nice cars, eaten at very nice restaurants. But superyacht rich is a whole different level. And if you're superyacht rich then you don't just go in the sea like the rest of us, have a paddle, get a pedalo. You don't even hire a nice little private boat. You take your beautiful yacht to a deserted stretch off the Mexican coast. Then you go and hunt fish, then take them back to your superyacht where you

56

make sashimi.* So one year, in between Christmas and New Year, that's where I found myself.

With spearfishing, you're not diving with a tank. You're emptying your lungs and diving down as far as you can. It's all a bit extreme sport and the two men I'm on the sailing yacht with are into that whole testing yourself against nature thing. And I obviously can't let myself back down. So one night, they suggest that the next morning we go spearfishing.

They're good swimmers and good divers, whereas the closest I've been to water that year was driving over the Thames on the way to work. It's December, so the water isn't exactly warm. I've never minded cold water. I've never been the sort of person who would volunteer to have a cold shower, but if there's cold water and I need to jump in and swim in it, then I will. There's this dinghy that comes out the back of the sailing yacht and the third mate on the yacht takes you out in it. So, we go out towards this stunningly beautiful reef. No one around us for a hundred miles as far as I can tell. Just the mountains we had watched go from a deep red to a purple as the sun set the night before.

So we're out and we're wearing these 'rashies, which are thin dive suits that stop you getting stung by jellyfish but don't do much against the cold. No breathing apparatus, just a mask and a snorkel, a spear gun and a weight belt (not that I really needed one). And I watch them go off the side of the boat. And all I can think is that there are loads of seals about. And I know enough to know that any time you have lots of seals in this part of the world you're going to get sharks.† And you get great whites in these parts. And the fish they're aiming to

---

* We're a long way from pints of maggots and an estuary in Essex.
† Sorry again, any sharks reading.

catch for sashimi are big old fish. You hit one of them with a spear and it bleeds and it thrashes about.

The two guys I'm with are regulars. They have all the latest gear, they're fit as can be. They know exactly what they're doing. I do not. They have these lures that bring in the little fish and the idea is that the little fish then bring in bigger fish until you get the size of fish you want to spear. I just want to be back on that beautiful yacht. But I can barely see it on the horizon. Instead, I'm about to jump into freezing, shark-infested waters, dressed, to all intents and purposes, like a large seal. But because of male pride and not wanting to look a wimp, I go in.

It's cold. Very cold. Jellyfish eggs immediately start to sting my forehead. The guys dive straight down to the reef, holding their breath for minutes at a time. I can barely get down deep enough to see a fish. Eventually I do spear one, but the third mate's expression lets me know what he thinks about its unimpressive size. Bouncing about in an inflatable dinghy for another three hours isn't my idea of a holiday, so I decide I'm going back to the yacht. I try to tell him that I'm going to fin to the boat, but if I don't make it, I'll head to those rocks.

But he just shakes his head, not understanding. At this point, I know nothing about boats. I haven't really thought about the fact that it took us half an hour to get out there in the dinghy.

'The boat,' I say. 'I'm going to head back to the boat. If I don't make it, I'll head towards those rocks and wait there. The rocks.'

He just nods. So I set off. Now, being a bit more of an experienced diver, I know that what I was trying to do was utterly stupid. Swim five nautical miles against an outgoing tide. But it doesn't look far away and it's still only about ten in the morning, so off I head. I'm so stupid, I take my spear gun with me. I'm finning for a couple of hours, and I don't seem to be getting much closer to the boat. I'm counting to a hundred and checking I'm still heading in the right direction. But I can see it, because its mast is absolutely enormous. I decide to head to the rocks and I'll wait there. It was only later I found out the 'rocks' I could see were about sixty feet of sheer straight rock and completely unclimbable.

So then I hear the engine from the dinghy heading back to the yacht. And I whistle as loudly as I can. But they can't hear me.

The third mate, in his bad English, has told them I've swum back. When they arrive, everyone has had their lunch and gone for a nap. So they assume that's where I must be.

Meanwhile I'm finning my heart out. I must be about five and a half hours in by this point and I'm not sure if I'm seeing things but these two seals come along and swim by me. And that's the last thing I want, because the seals are going to attract the sharks. And I am by far the biggest seal, so top of the menu. So I start telling them, 'Sod off. Sod off, seals.' But the more I tell them to sod off, the more they think I'm playing and they start to frolic.

I'm finning away from them, but they seem to have decided I'm one of them, so they keep swimming closer. At one point a swordfish comes and has a look and then zooms away. I'm getting a bit closer but I'm still not making enough headway.

Later I will learn that this is the moment they finally realise I'm not on the boat. But all I know at that point is that I hear an outboard motor again but it doesn't come towards me, it goes off towards the rocks. The rocks where I said I'd be.

So I'm splashing and whistling. They're sporadically turning off the motor and every time they do, I'm waving and whistling. And that's when I realised that from where they are, I probably look quite a lot like a seal.

The sun is really sinking now and I know they won't be able to find me when it gets dark. I'm starting to think that this might really be it. But then suddenly the sound of the motor is a lot louder and they're pulling me out of the water. And that's when I realise I'm still wearing my weight belt and holding my spear gun. I'm stung and sunburned and my mouth is so dry I can't speak. They give me water and we head back to the yacht. They fix me up with a plate of sashimi and plenty of water. Then plenty more beer. And gradually it becomes a funny story. But I promise I am never going spearfishing again. This lasts for exactly one year.

About a year later, I'm on a superyacht again, off another astonishingly beautiful coastline, Australia this time.* Do I want to go spearfishing? I am understandably wary but again, I can't be the whinging pom. And this time I'm with an expert. They have brought a world champion spearfisherman to accompany us. He has a lure made of two bits of interlocking mirror that shines and attracts the right sort of fish. He is basically Aqua Man. It's like Lewis Hamilton taking you out for your first driving lesson. And of course, I can't say no.

Now I haven't had much time to practise my spearfishing in the preceding year, and because I'm kind of tagging along, I've got the slightly duff equipment; the equivalent of the stuff left in the PE cupboard. I've got the wrong sort of fins – the sort with straps on – and I've got a spear gun that's fitted with the wrong sort of line. You're meant to have line that floats

_____

* I know, the sheer bloody grind of it all.

to the surface, so it doesn't get wrapped around things like the straps on your fins. So I'm feeling like a bit of a disaster waiting to happen.

We're in there for about an hour before the world champion spearfisher shouts to me that there's a Spanish mackerel, and I look down and this isn't like any mackerel I've ever seen. This isn't like the mackerel we used to hook in Norfolk. This is about three foot long and looks like it's been on steroids for several years. So I take a shot and by some miracle I shoot it down through the dorsal fin. So now I've got to kill it. I've got this fish under my arm. 'Put the knife in its eye and wiggle it about.' But it's a big old fish and I can't get hold of it properly. And then I hear him say, 'Kill the fish. There's reefies.' And I look down and I can see the sharks circling about coming upwards. This is a very laid-back guy and I hear, for the first time a note of urgency in his voice and I can see the line wrapped around the straps of my fins and I don't want to think what might happen if it decides to make a break for deep water and pulls me down with it. So it's bleeding and thrashing about and he's a bit louder and more urgent when he says, 'Kill the fish now.' And my weight belt is dragging me down. He's telling me to kill the fish. I'm trying to say 'I'm trying to kill the fish' but all that comes out is 'I'm blooble, ooble, the fubble fish.'

But I get my knife and I stick it in and I'm wiggling the knife about. And this time he says, 'Kill the fish right now.' And I look down and a reef shark comes up and bumps against my fin. I have a weird moment when I thought that sharks are fish too and they're probably annoyed at me for hurting one of their fish mates. The Spanish mackerel stops thrashing, and we climb up into the dinghy with me expecting something to take a chunk out of me at any minute.

Funnily enough they never invited me back and I made myself a promise I wasn't going back in the water again for a very long time.

Shipwrecked

I never thought I'd find myself kneeling on a shipping container fifteen metres below the water in a quarry (sorry, dive centre) just outside of Heathrow, as pieces of scaffolding were thrown down to me on a bowline to assemble underwater. Then taking it apart, tying it to a bowline and yanking it for them to pull it back up again. There are times in my life when my three years at drama school have served me well, but this wasn't one of them. I couldn't help wondering why I wasn't in a trailer eating a bacon sandwich and waiting to go in the makeup chair.

I've been asked to do all sorts of things over the years.* These have ranged from playing an Oompa-Loompa to fielding a number of indecent proposals. But I couldn't turn down the chance to genuinely dive for buried treasure. My inner child would never forgive me. I read the treatment for what became *Shipwreck Treasure Hunter* and it just seemed like a unique opportunity to take audiences somewhere we never normally get to see.

And I didn't know it at the time but my family tree is planted in salt water. As part of the research for the show, I learned that my great-great-grandfather came over from Ireland and owned a barge company, which he sold and used

---

* Though, annoyingly, never my dream part: the MC in *Cabaret*.

the proceeds to buy a pub called the Ship and Castle, which is still in Portsmouth Harbour. Their family was so large – fifteen children – they had to have dinner in shifts because they couldn't all fit around the table. When they needed a bath, they'd get thrown out of windows in the harbour. My great-grandfather, Pop (named after Popeye), first went to sea when he was ten and would spend large parts of his life there for the next fifty years, and he was shipwrecked three times. Whenever I'd been left floating in the sea multiple times, I'd clearly been carrying on a family tradition.

But then there was the gruelling process of getting the HSE qualifications that would let me make the show, which ended in learning from legendary dive master Neil Brock (one of the funniest and toughest blokes I've ever met). There aren't many presenters in the country who have this qualification. I trained nearly every day for two months, with a five-hour written paper at the end. I'm far from being a good diver but I love it. People die every year in UK waters; they are dangerous. Sometimes you get down there and you can just about see your hand in front of your face. There's so much sediment. You can't read your depth gauge on your wrist. There are times when we're a tiny bit out with our calculations – for instance if your shot line narrowly misses the wreck and you land on the seabed, the ship could be so close you could reach out and touch it, but the visibility is so bad you can't see it. You feel like you may as well be in outer space. It can be an eerie environment.

There's an amazing feeling of camaraderie and discovery with the crew we work with. There's a rhyme Neil taught me about how to cut a line underwater: 'Always cut towards your chum. Never cut towards your thumb. You can always get another chum but you can never get another thumb.'

What I love about *Shipwreck* is that it's a history programme that doesn't feel like it. History can often appear quite intangible and abstract on television. You can do reconstructions or dramatise moments but often, to inject a bit of pace, you're left with that same old formula of a historian walking through a historical setting shouting about what happened. When you're diving on the wrecks it's this privileged experience of being able to reach out and literally touch history. It's shaking hands with ghosts. You're encountering things that haven't been seen since the ship sank. If history can often be a bit dry, this very much isn't.*

Though I'm with experts, I am very much not one. You see me finding all sorts of things out and learning. Until we made the programme, I wasn't aware of the relationship between British businessmen and the Confederacy during the American Civil War; they were selling them British-made ships to use as blockade runners. And I went and dived on one. If we hadn't sold them those ships and guns, the civil war might have been over years earlier. We did one dive on a former slave ship in Plymouth Harbour and found the cannons that were designed to turn inwards to be used against the enslaved people on board.

I think it's incredibly important to look all parts of our history in the eye. When I was a kid, the connection between British ports and slavery was glossed over. I'm someone who believes that, where British history is concerned, there are good things that should be celebrated and there are bad things that we need to acknowledge and learn from.

I've never been interested in just knowing things for knowing's sake. I want information that equips me to understand and do things differently in the future.

---

* Sorry, couldn't help myself.

If you'd told eighteen-year-old-me that I'd be squealing with excitement finding a bit of copper from a nineteenth-century frigate, I'd never have believed you.

But I think if you'd explained to that kid in the bath, making icebergs out of fairy liquid that one day, he'd be diving down on actual shipwrecks, shaking hands with history, he'd have got it.

There's just always been something about me and water.

Don't Give a Monkey's

'Water, water, please,' I gasp into the phone, dehydrated.
I've been in hospital for the better part of eleven days,
where for a long time I have been delirious and seeing four
tiny monkeys, two on my shoulders and two on my ankles
screeching in this kind of Punch and Judy voice, 'I'm really
really hot' and another replying, 'You think you're hot?!
Well, I'm melting.'

'Is that you, Grant?' says a deep voice. 'Nah, you're all right,
Grant. You're on my manor now.'

I am thirty-five years old and I *really* need water. It's all
down to the humble mosquito.* In subsequent years I will be
bitten by an international who's who of mosquitos. From the
special force mosquitos of Afghanistan, through the rich array
present in Africa, South and Central America and Southeast
Asia, all the way to the giant ones in Alaska† – I've been hit
by a swarm of mosquitos at a watering hole in the Arizona
desert, where the swarm followed us into the Sheriff's car and
we smacked them onto the ceiling until our own blood dripped
onto our heads. My poor head has been left looking like the

---

* It's the opposite of sharks. The mosquito is the world's deadliest animal.
Along with flies that carry disease they're responsible for millions of deaths
a year.
† By all rights, the national bird of Alaska should really be the mosquito.

surface of the moon. But back then I was far less acquainted with them.

I was standing for Rector of the University of Glasgow. I'd been asked by good friends Margaret McDonagh and Waheed Alli and, to be honest, I didn't fully understand quite how involved or contentious a role it was going to be. Despite the occasional protest and some bags of flour being thrown, I got the gig.

So at one point, I had to go up and give a speech to the students and I had to meet the press. I hadn't been feeling terrific for a few days, but I was up there campaigning, when in the middle of talking to a journalist my teeth started chattering uncontrollably and he immediately said, 'Have you been to Africa recently?'

'Yes,' I chattered. I'd recently returned from a photographic safari in Kenya.

'You might have malaria.'

'I don't think so.'

And then my mind flew back to the times my girlfriend and I had been camping when my girlfriend had thought it was a good idea for me to get out from under the mosquito net and go and proactively kill them, in case they got into the mosquito net. So if I spotted a big one, I'd get out from under the net and I'd go and get it.* Clearly one of them had taken their revenge. I also thought back to my decision that I didn't need to take my antimalarials for as long as I was supposed to after I'd got back.† But I've got a plane to catch so I head to the airport, chattering all the way. And my girlfriend's mother is staying with us and she takes one look at me when I get back

---

* Hint: don't do this.
† Hint: really don't do this.

and she says, 'Jesus, Ross, you don't look good.' And I don't feel good either, so I go to bed.

And as the night goes on, I'm not only sweating and shivering and my teeth can't stop chattering, I'm now delirious too. Apparently, I was calling all sorts of things out. In the morning, I call my doctor and he says it definitely sounds like malaria. But to test for it, you need to be having a flare-up and the parasite needs to be active in your system to be detectable. If it happens again, give this hospital a ring and explain you need to come in. So that night, as before when my teeth start chattering, I give the hospital a ring. But I get the night porter.

'Hello, this is Ross Kemp, I need to come in I've got malaria.'

'What, Grant Mitchell?'

'No, I'm Ross Kemp. I'm really sick, I need to . . .'

'I've got Grant Mitchell here, giving it the big'un. That's not very tough, is it.'

Then he put the phone down. I just sat there, astonished, and said out loud, 'Did that just happen?'

The next morning, I head into the hospital. And it all goes downhill quickly. It isn't long before the paparazzi turn up and, over the next few days, I can tell how ill I am by how many of them are there. When things are bad, more and more turn up. But when they drift away, I'm clearly getting better.

During the worst of it, I couldn't walk. I had to be carried to the toilet. I don't remember about four days of my life. I was too weak to lift my arms.

I was sweating so much, they had plastic sheets and used to just roll me to the side and scoop the sweat off the sheets with a kidney bowl. I would be so cold that the duvet lifting an inch would feel like someone was blasting me with freezing air. Any sort of draught was like a spear of ice. I lost about a stone in a week. Then my body temperature would spike. And that's when the monkeys would appear. Most nights they would be chattering at me. I was so out of it, I'd just nod. *Oh, the monkeys are back.*

After a while, I felt a little bit better and I would wake up thirsty. I was well enough to take myself to the toilet for a bit. You could push this button and a nurse would come in and bring water. So I push it but nothing happens. Then I ring the nurse's station and they pick up the phone, and a familiar voice says, 'Is that you, Grant?'

'Can I have some water?'

'You're on my manor now.'

And then I just lost it. I start getting out of bed and I don't care if I can barely walk, I'm going to stumble down there with my bum hanging out the back of my hospital gown and I'm going to have a few words with him.

But my girlfriend beats me to it. She calms me down and tells me she'll deal with it. She comes down the corridor and she can hear him speaking on the phone, feet up on the desk. The night porter: 'Yeah, mate, I just told Grant Mitchell he's on my manor.'

Unfortunately for him, one of the nurses heard him too and he didn't last long in that job.

I don't care how much you don't like Grant Mitchell, it was me who wanted the glass of water.

To be honest, it was probably a good thing for both of us that I didn't get to him.

Fashion Victim

'Oi, get him!'

I am seventeen years old, dressed as a New Romantic, walking through the car park of Shenfield train station late one night, on my way back from a night of dancing at Zhivago's in Southend with my girlfriend, when I hear a bloke shout and see three figures running towards me. I was taking a shortcut through the car park, which had become a place where men who objected to men loving men would hang about hoping to be violent towards them.

Time to leg it. The only trouble is the outfit I'm wearing, which includes a cummerbund and a pleated white shirt, a leather knee-length rain mac, shiny black plastic trousers and velvet Revelle pirate-style boots with no grip.* It's wintertime and there's still piles of snow and slush and ice everywhere, but I set off running, slipping about on my heels, slightly worrying about what the water is going to do to the velvet. I'm playing rugby for my county at this point, so in spite of everything, I open up a decent distance between us and settle into a nice easy rhythm towards home.

I've always been into fashion. No one ever expects me to be. Either they've got that Grant Mitchell uniform of jeans

---

* If you're imaging Grant dressed as a New Romantic, think again. I effectively have a curly quiff with blonde highlights in it. Sadly no more.

and a leather jacket in their head, or they're thinking of when I do a documentary and I'm wearing the same black T-shirt and trousers. But that's just for continuity, it means that whether it's a walking shot or a driving shot, I just wear the same T-shirt and trousers (the same type, not the exact ones). It also hides all the sweat and mud and everything else too. But whenever I've had the money, I've liked to spend it on clothes. I certainly don't do it now – I dread to think how much I've spent over the years and I'm sure there are times I've looked like a right knob, but I've always felt it's an extension of your personality. And at this stage, as I skidded around the corner onto the main road, that meant full-on New Romantic.

I was always pretty eclectic with music and fashion. Bruce Lee was one of my heroes growing up. My nan used to work in the printing place for these Kung Fu magazines. So I'd get all these pictures of Bruce Lee in amazing shirts and suits and sunglasses. He was very cool. A fashion icon.

And fashion was so tied to music at the time. My parents listened to lots of different music, especially when we were driving to our camping holidays – Sinatra, Elvis and Johnny Mathis and Nat King Cole, Nina Simone and the Beatles and the Rolling Stones too. I grew up without any kind of distinction between music and the different sorts of people who had made it. It was all just music.

I have a vivid memory of listening to 'Ballroom Blitz' by Sweet on my mum and dad's Philips cassette recorder in the caravan when I was maybe ten or eleven. I was thirteen in 1977 and there were definitely a few of us at school who thought it would be fun to be Johnny Rotten, ripping an old T-shirt up and drawing on it. And of course all the cool older kids were properly into punk, constantly gobbing at each other.

There was an outbreak of the Russian flu in 1977, which I'm pretty sure wasn't helped by all the gobbing.

And then I got into heavy metal for a bit. I had dreams of setting up a band for a while and there are photographs of me with long, curly hair holding a guitar I couldn't play. Then for a little while I decided I wanted to be a mod and cut my hair short and started wearing Hush Puppies and my dad's two-tone suits that didn't fit him anymore. That wasn't the cleverest thing to do as at this point you had to hope you didn't bump into any skinheads or rockers. I didn't have a scooter but I had the suit. I bought *Jazz* by Queen and I bought *No More Heroes* by the Stranglers on the same day. But I was just as into Chic and Motown. I was obsessed with *The Blues Brothers* when it came out, me and my brother watched it so many times we wore the tape out on the VHS.

I wanted to apply for drama schools. In response the careers person at school said that I should go and work in Topman in Bond Street. I'm not sure if this was some elaborate preparation for being an actor, or a comment on my acting (or my dress sense), but either way my mum and I definitely weren't on board with that. So instead my mum found this drama course at Southend Tech and it was a two-year course. With the help of Dot Feakins, I prepared two pieces for them and Kate and Don, who ran the course, said I could go straight into the second year. I knew I wanted to go to drama school as early as possible. I wonder if me wanting to see so much of the world now was because I went to drama school so young. I ended up leaving drama school when I was only twenty.

Southend opened up a whole different world to me, I spent my days doing dance and drama and movement. I had curly hair with a headband, grey legwarmers. The full *Fame* look.

I had my eye on the prize that I was going to audition for one of the five major drama schools, which were really difficult to get into and then I knew I needed a grant, which was even harder. I had a girlfriend at the time who would catch the train back with me from Southend. These were the days of separate carriages with doors and we worked out there was about a twenty-minute stretch with no stations where we'd definitely have the carriage to ourselves, we had a ticket to ride and we'd take the opportunity if we could.

I started going regularly to Zhivago's, which was the place to be if you were into New Romantic music, which I was, along with all sorts of other music.

I've always loved to dance too. My mum and dad were always dancers.* They met at a Valentine's Day dance when they were fifteen or sixteen. I was always encouraged to dance. It's served me well over the years. It helps in so many things, sports, martial arts, to be able to find that rhythm and move along to it. I've danced with tribesmen on the plains of Madagascar, with their prized zebu (cows), I've danced to baile funk in the favelas of Brazil, done some deep griding in Nairobi nightclubs. Wherever I've been around the world, it's a great way to have fun, release and occasionally make new friends. It just needs someone to start a beat and then to show you're willing to join in and enjoy yourself. There are times when it's probably not a good idea – I wouldn't recommend you start bouncing around with gang members in Chicago, but most of the time, if you show you're up for it, get involved and not just sit and watch, people respond. I think it's a fundamental human impulse to fear putting yourself out there and risk people laughing at you for trying.

---

* They still are, in their mid-eighties.

I've always regretted not standing up and dancing, over the times I have and someone's laughed.*

But I'm not really thinking about any of this as I slip along in my suede boots. Instead, I start to wonder why I'm running away at all. I had boxed for my county and was playing rugby for my county. It looks like there are only three of them, so I decide to change strategy. I stop running and I turn round and shout out, 'Well, come on then!' As loudly as I can. And they skid to a halt and just stand there.

Then I hear a voice go 'Ross?'

And I go, 'Yeah.'

And one of them holds his hand up and says, 'Sorry, mate, didn't realise it was you.' And they sheepishly head back towards the train station, and I carry on my walk home.

Although it took me ages to get the salt stains out of my boots, at least I didn't end up an actual fashion victim and lived to dance another day.

---

*   This is not a plea to be on *Strictly*.

Dame Kemp

It's never a good sign when the entire pub breaks into applause and wolf whistles when you come in. But I realised quite quickly what had happened.

I was thirty-three years old. It was a Thursday night in November, and I had spent the last couple of hours rugby training. I'd spent the day going through my lines for a part in a show called *City Central*, which was one of the first things I did after leaving *EastEnders*. I was going to be in an episode called 'Nothing Like a Dame' where I played the part of Dilly Dally, a drag queen in Manchester.

At this point I was living in a house in the same road as my first girlfriend, about a five-minute walk from the porch I'd demolished. This was the house that had the Grant Mitchell *Spitting Image* puppet up in the window, which we set up with its back to the window, so it always looked like I was in. I got back from rugby training with a plan to meet a couple of the lads in the Green Dragon, that night, which meant I had a few hours to work on Dilly.

I'd taken my muddy shirt and shorts off but kept my neoprene bottoms on. I'm pretty sure I kept my rugby socks on too. I'd been sent the costume and given these high heels and I knew I needed to practise walking in them or it was going to look terrible. Channelling Mrs Feakins from all those years before, I knew, if my character wore heels, then I needed to look like I wore heels. I didn't want to look like I'd only put them on that morning. So I decided to go out into the extension where I'd be able to watch my reflection and check I was doing it right. I was confident that no one could see into the back garden because of the hedges all around.

In one scene at a club, I have to do a song, 'I Will Survive' by Gloria Gaynor. So I bring the cassette player out and I play the song and I'm practising the steps and the dancing, bare-chested, in my neoprene bottoms, rugby socks and heels. I am *going* for it, hairbrush (not mine, obviously) for a microphone, kicking out my hips, belting it out with my best Manchester accent. I get to the end and then I re-start the song and go again. I do it again, and again, until I feel like I've got hold of it, like I'll be able to do it at the rehearsal.

And then I go up and grab a shower before wandering down to the pub, humming Gloria Gaynor, thinking about the part. Push open the door to the pub. And that's when the whistles start.

It turned out that in winter the hedges were not the impermeable barrier I thought they were and one of my neighbours had spotted me. Apparently you could hear me several streets away. He'd told someone, who had told someone, who filmed it on their camera phone, who had shown the pub.

There was nothing else to do but bow and accept the whistles. There ain't nothing like a dame.

Barbara

'Dame Barbara Windsor, MBE, not a bad epitaph for a girl from Stoke Newington.' That was how I began the eulogy I was truly honoured to be asked to give by Barbara's husband, Scott, at her funeral service. It was an extremely moving day and a fitting tribute to a woman who'd led such a rich life. It took me days to get it right, as I wanted to try and capture what was so special about her. I could barely get through reading it, because it brought back so many intense memories of her. The term national treasure gets used a lot, but she truly was. I was lucky enough to know her for over twenty-five years.

Barbara would tell a story, which I didn't tell in her eulogy but which I think of often. She had been a starlet in the sixties. And in London, that meant you were going to spend time around gangsters. She'd hung around with the Krays and been married to Ronnie Knight, who owned nightclubs and would later see prison for handling money from a big bank job.

She told me she'd once been advised that you should never start a fight you weren't prepared to finish. So when she got into a disagreement with a woman in a nightclub and things were becoming a touch heated, she picked up a barstool in order to make good on the advice. The problem was, of course, that she was less than five foot tall and quite top heavy.* So she lifted up the barstool and when it reached a certain height, she fell slowly backwards on her very high heels.

Then she would laugh. She was never happier than when she was laughing at herself. Actually, that's a piece of genuine life advice: if you become famous for your laugh, you'll know you've had a good life.

A few years beforehand, Scott and I had made a documentary about dementia together. By that time Barbara wasn't well enough to be in it but she wanted people to know that they weren't alone. There are 700,000 people caring for 850,000 people with dementia. It's the biggest killer in the UK and we don't have a cure for it. As many as 70 per cent of all people in care homes have dementia. By 2050, one in three of us will have it. I believe wholeheartedly we need to view it as a medical care issue, not a social care issue. It was a film that I felt especially passionate about.

Scott's surname is Mitchell and when he was about to leave drama school, he realised there was already an actor called Scott Mitchell, so he changed his name to Grant Mitchell. The only problem was that this was in early 1990, literally the week before Grant Mitchell the character appeared in *EastEnders* and someone pointed out to him that if he wanted to be an actor playing all sorts of different parts, this probably wasn't the best stage name to have. So he changed it back to Scott Mitchell. Barbara used to joke that she couldn't get away from Mitchells anywhere she went.

We had all met coincidentally for the first time about six months before she joined *EastEnders* when we were both doing

---

* Because of the difference in height between us, Barbara would often film her scenes behind the bar standing on a beer crate.

a surreal charity event, which involved us riding a white stretch limo through parts of Glasgow. Over the years, she would be my go-to person. She was my confidante. We trusted each other. I saw more of her during those years than I did of my actual family. She was very dear to me. The day I left Albert Square, we did a photocall and for both of us it was a real moment. To realise that we wouldn't see each other every day any more. We were both crying. If you were out with her, it would take ages to get anywhere. People would stop in the street to tell her how much she meant to them. She'd have a kind word for everyone, would stop and speak for as long as it took. She had known so many different types of people and she could talk on any subject. She was so sharp and wickedly funny. It didn't matter what we were talking about, one of us would pull a face and then we'd both start giggling. She was from the East End and I was from Essex and we just got each other, I think. She was a joy to be around.

Scott told me he first realised she was becoming ill when that joy began to diminish. She'd had the most incredible life and she retained this youthful energy, but she was becoming less and less able to remember that life. Those glimpses of who she was became less and less frequent. I went round to see her and there were reminders up on the wall 'You are Dame Barbara Windsor', 'This is where you live', 'You are married to Scott', 'He loves you'. We would have a long conversation where she seemed to know me and then she'd look away, look back at me and say, 'Who are you?' And she was gone again.

Barbara was a brilliant storyteller, and it never mattered that you'd heard some of them before. There'd be the punchline and that laugh, always with perfect timing. So it was noticeable when that started to change. She had to rely on Scott more to fill in for her. Then she went for a series of tests and scans, and they found out she had Alzheimer's.

Scott told me that when Barbara told him the diagnosis, she apologised to him. I knew how much they loved each other and that got me.

Barbara decided she had to leave *EastEnders* before she'd told anyone about her illness. I got ambushed by her one day on holiday in Mallorca. She called me up and asked what I was doing the following week. I said I was on holiday with my family in Mallorca. She said, 'Oh, we'll be there too. Let's meet for lunch.' (Like you do.) She was always up for lunch and a gossip and a giggle. She let me know that she was going to leave the show, but she didn't tell me why. She loved the show so much and she said she wanted Grant to be part of Peggy's goodbye storyline. For the character and for the viewers.

I was in the middle of an extremely full-on series of documentaries. I'd been in Columbia, then Iraq and Syria, then Mozambique and then Mongolia. So dropping Walford into that felt like one ingredient too many. However, when Barbara asked you for something, you had to say yes. But I felt a bit nervous going back. I'd got off the plane from Mozambique and was jet-lagged. I didn't want to let people down, especially Barbara. But luckily there was a kind of muscle memory that came back immediately. Working with Steve and working with Letitia. Going back to that square where I spent a decade of my life. But it was strange too. Like nothing had changed and everything, especially considering where I'd just been.

On the day of Barbara's funeral, I was looking for a pen to make some final revisions to the eulogy. I reached up to the top shelf of a cupboard and there was this piece of card. When I lifted it down, I saw: 'To my darling Ross, thank you. Lots of love, Bar.' It was from a bunch of flowers Barbara had sent me once. I'd clearly wanted to save the message, had put it up there to keep it safe and then forgot about it. It was just a coincidence, but I felt very close to her memory in that moment.

I'm truly thankful that I'll always have Scott as a close friend. And Barbara, I miss you dreadfully.

Tiger Tiger

'You're looking in the mirror,' says the plummy, husky-voiced man.

Seventeen-year-old me nods, doing my best to mime a man looking in the mirror. Because I know that the man sitting behind this desk in Chelmsford County Hall asking me to do it holds the key to my future as an actor. Through some mystical process, if I impress him, he will approve my grant to go to drama school, which means I will be able to afford the fees. This was in the middle of Margaret Thatcher's premiership and her government were aggressively cutting grants to the arts. There were only a handful of them for thousands of applications.

I'd had two recalls from RADA, one from Central and a no from everyone else. I'd also had an offer from Guildford, which I didn't want to go to because I had my heart set on going to live in London. My one London offer was from Webber Douglas, but at this point if I don't get the grant, I can't afford to go. So this man holds the key to my future, which, to the contrary of all available evidence, seventeen-year-old me believes will involve being on television.

'You're looking in the mirror,' he says, fixing me in the eye. 'Perhaps you're shaving, perhaps you're brushing your teeth.' I dutifully begin to mime shaving my imaginary beard away, pulling the skin taut, lifting my chin (though I hadn't actually started shaving for real at this point).

In the waiting room is this year's crop of youngsters from Essex who want to go into the performing arts. There are people with various instrument cases, people wearing ballet outfits. And as far as I can see, we're all coming in to see the same panel of three people, who seem to be the authority for every type of performing art in Essex. And this guy, who was straight out of central casting for ex-actor, seemed to be the key to all things dramatic. I have no idea what pathway led him to be one of the gatekeepers to all artistic dreams in Essex. Maybe he was just a bloke from the finance office who went to the theatre the most. But I am acting my soul out at him. I'd done my monologue from *Under Milk Wood* and speech from *The Tempest* at him to no real discernible reaction. So I know I need to show him I'm taking this seriously. I am miming shaving as hard as anyone ever has. I'm cleaning the razor in the water to get rid of the bristles and foam. I'm turning my face in the imaginary mirror to spot every last stray bit of stubble.

'And then . . .' Plummy husky-voiced man leans forward. I pause mid-shave. 'And then you look into the shaving mirror and you see . . . you see, a TIGER sitting in your bath!' he bellows.

I look at him, just to check I've heard him right. 'What do you do?' His eyes are wide.

To this day, I don't know what face I pulled, or, indeed, what face one should pull to communicate there is a tiger behind you in your bathroom.* But I got the grant, the first grant that changed my life (and without it there would never have been the second one).

To this day, I can't hear the word tiger without hearing it in that plummy, husky voice gone high-pitched with excite-

---

* Though years later I would find myself in a cage with a lion in Munich.

ment, without thinking of his wide eyes, his hands gesturing frantically for me to begin my performance as the shaving man who sees a tiger.

That Could Be Your Head

'What's wrong?' Andrew Riddel, the owner of one of the country's biggest privately owned zoos, is looking at me strangely. 'I was just asking if you wanted to come see the pelt of my favourite tiger and you pulled a face.' It was a fair cop.

'Long story, mate. Yes, let's go see your favourite tiger.'

If I'm being completely honest, I don't massively want to go and see his tiger's pelt, but it's 2020 and we're making a documentary about people who have dangerous wild animal licenses and keep exotic animals in the UK.* Andrew had a private zoo over a 46-acre site in Lincolnshire, housing more than 235 animals, including zebras, camels, wolves and lions. In spite of my feelings about people who keep animals in zoos full stop, I couldn't help but like Andrew. I do think that many of the animals that he kept would have died if he hadn't been there.

He'd made his zoo from scrap metal. The bars came from Lincoln prison when it was being refurbished. It was an impressive set-up. He had more land than London Zoo.

He drives me slightly too fast in his Bentley GT out to an old windswept church on the edge of the Lincolnshire fens that had

---

* Honestly you would not believe how many people do. Some estimates are as high as 4000 wild animals. The one that got me was the astonishing number of people who own wolves.

been converted into a taxidermist's studio. And there's stuffed animals everywhere. Every sort you can think of. Even the taxidermist looked slightly cadaverous. As we walk through, I keep thinking the animals hanging from the ceiling are moving.

So we get to the skin of the tiger and he's stroking it and telling me how much he loved that tiger, looking me in the eye intensely, 'Even though you couldn't go near him and he wanted to kill you every second.'

For the same documentary, I met a man called Gary who kept forty-three snakes in his terraced house in Derby. And bear in mind this was not a large house. I was looking at it from the outside and wondering how he kept any snakes in there. And it turned out he'd got Tupperware boxes full of snakes in a converted airing cupboard. Apparently every now and then one of them would escape up into the roof and scare the bejesus out of the nice Polish lady next door. Some of these snakes were 10 feet long. At one point, an albino labyrinth Burmese python wrapped itself around my legs and I was very grateful when it wasn't there anymore.

Gary has converted one of the bedrooms upstairs, installing a paddling pool and a platform with a ladder on it. And that's Thor's room. Thor is a massive monitor lizard who Gary takes for walks on a lead. There's only one room just for humans and that's the downstairs lounge. One night, Thor chewed through his paddling pool water pipe and the whole thing came down through the ceiling. When we leave after a few hours of filming with Gary, I'm gobsmacked when I glance up and Thor is looking out of the upstairs window of his terraced house at us. I couldn't help feeling that both of us were in the wrong place.

Back at Andrew's private zoo, they have four lions in two enclosures; his partner, Tracy, puts down a couple of pigs' heads and various other animal parts. They release the lions and one of them goes straight to the nearest pig's head and starts crunching on it like it's a gobstopper. And she looks across and in her deep Lincolnshire accent she says, 'That could be your head, that could be.'

Sometimes you don't need words. My look said it all.

Karachi Morgue

'These ones do not have a head.' The man in charge of the morgue is showing us around and I see that, he is absolutely right, they don't. Later this will be pixelated out in the footage for the film. But there are no pixels in real life.

I am forty-eight and we're making a film in Karachi about the war being waged for control of the city. Later, we will be shot at on the rooftop while meeting Uzair Baloch. But right now, as so often happens, we're in a morgue. The bodies have their faces showing, so people can come to the morgue and claim them. There's such a constant flow of new bodies that, if they aren't claimed within a week, the morgue will bury them.

This is not one of those gleaming, ice-cold morgues you see on the television. This is chipped paint, improvised surfaces with bodies piled up and covered in stained sheets. Some of them are from traffic accidents. This is what happens when the mechanisms for dealing with death become utterly over-whelmed. Everybody that comes through is given a number and the number tracked, so at least someone would one day be able to work out where their loved one was.

The smell of human death is quite particular. While making a film about ivory poaching, we found the decomposing carcass of an elephant that had died a slow death at the hands of poachers and was covered in guano, and that was pretty bad, but to my mind it's not as bad as the smell of a rotting person.

89

There's something about it that feels noxious, overwhelming. You have to be a special sort of person to spend your days immersed in it. At one point in the morgue, I was doing a piece to camera and somebody thought it would be funny to lock us in. For what felt like hours, but was probably only minutes, me and the cameraman were banging on the door, and they left us in there. I won't ever forget what it was like being in there – the bodies with their mouths open and their arms stretched outwards by rigor mortis, as if they were calling out to you for help. I can still close my eyes and be straight back there.

We wanted to see what happened when one of the bodies was taken to be buried, which meant meeting an incredible man called Dr Edhi, who ran a charitable welfare organisation that rescued abandoned women and children, ran orphanages, rural welfare clinics and shelters. It also ran a voluntary ambulance service with 1800 ambulances across the country.

He was famously ascetic, owning only two sets of clothes. Every day he ate lunch with the poor on the streets of Karachi.

Those who volunteer for the Edhi ambulance service work for £1 a day, often for 24-hour shifts, picking up the injured. But one of their roles was also to ferry the unclaimed bodies out to where they are buried. The drivers chewed betel nut and spoke quickly, operating at a manic speed. They had been pressed into service to deal with the aftermath of the gang violence in places like Lyari. One of the drivers told me he would never forget what he had seen and would be woken up most nights by bad dreams.

So we went with them as they took an unclaimed body out to be buried. In the film, you see me getting into the Edhi Foundation combi van with him. And then the next shot is him being buried. But what actually happened was that I travelled across Karachi in the van. The corpse, wrapped in cloth, was put in the back, directly behind me.

What I didn't realise was that, in Karachi traffic, 'just across the city' can take three and a half hours. But off we go. It's in the high thirties as we're driving and I immediately start dripping with sweat. The body, remember, hasn't come from a freezer. It's just been in a relatively cool room. And now it's in a very warm van. And there's no air conditioning. We have to make the decision whether we're going to suffocate from traffic fumes or from the smell in the van. We choose traffic fumes. We make it about two minutes before we hit the first traffic jam and I feel a 'thump' in my back. My first thought is 'he's still alive!' But then I turn around and realise that the body isn't actually that firmly secured. So every time the vehicle stops suddenly, it slides forward half a foot and his head hits me in the middle of the back. And he's starting to leak and I'm trying not to breathe through my nose.

For more than three hours, we keep jerking forward, with the body hitting me in the back every time we hit traffic or a set of lights (and there is a lot of traffic in Karachi). When we get out the other end, I ask the driver, 'Do you get used to this?'

He replies, 'No, you never get used to this.'

Covid

Another morgue. Another overwhelmed man looking me in the eyes.

But this time I'm in Milton Keynes. There can be a danger when you make the sort of film that I do that people think extreme things don't happen to people like them. But the events of 2019 and 2020 brought home to all of us just how wrong that assumption is.

We were filming at Milton Keynes University Hospital in March 2020. We'd wanted to make two films to show how the NHS was dealing with the pandemic. It took a lot of pushing to negotiate access, but it felt like we desperately needed to understand the human response to this extraordinary situation. To reassure the public that there were people doing everything possible to keep us safe. I have always had an enormous admiration for people who work in medicine. But it didn't start well.

One local newspaper printed a story about 'Ross Kemp sunning himself while patients die'. What had happened was that Johnny the director/cameraman and I had come out of our first time filming in the ICU.* And at that point, you put less PPE on to go into space than we did to go into ICU. We were in the ICU for less than an hour and it was an uncomfortable

---

* Johnny, it's a pleasure working with you. May the journey continue.

alien environment. There were people who were working fifteen-hour shifts in those conditions. They were watching hundreds of people die. They had to create a second ICU. You went into a ward full of intubated people, no one was awake. I remember seeing the worry in the doctor's eyes when he told me he had never seen anything like it. He was exhausted, his eyes rimmed with red, and they had tears in when he was asking people to think of those around them and stay home. He described it as like a war. His hospital was a field hospital. Hundreds of NHS workers died. They didn't have enough beds, they didn't have enough ventilators.

I think we've forgotten too quickly the debt we owe to those frontline workers in the NHS. When people want to talk about bravery, that is bravery. To be looking at the scenarios they were looking at and to carry on and do your job. To work twenty-hour days, in those conditions to try and help your fellow humans. That's what bravery looks like. The things those NHS workers did for us and our loved ones, should never ever be forgotten. I've often made films that take you into the heart of people who are capable of some dreadful things. But that was a truly great thing I witnessed. That was the very best of what human beings are capable of. It was an honour to be there and to witness that and to try and capture that and get it across to an audience at home. Because we were all scared and none of us knew what was going to happen, so to celebrate the bravery and selflessness of those workers felt like the absolute right thing to do.

So my director/cameraman Johnny and I come out of the ICU. We're emotional with what we've just seen. I hadn't been able to finish a piece to camera because I'd just cracked in the middle of it. My voice broke and I couldn't speak without starting to cry. We are decontaminated, take off the multiple layers of PPE, come out into the fresh air and we just lay down on our backs – this was after forty-five minutes, so I have no idea how those working shifts for hours managed. One of the nurses comes out with two cups of tea. I cannot get over the kindness of someone doing that. Of course someone took a photograph of us at that exact moment and it looked like we were sunning ourselves at a garden party, demanding to be waited on by nurses. The images attracted quite a lot of negative attention to begin with because, completely understandably, people who weren't allowed in to spend time with their ill relatives in hospital couldn't understand why we were allowed in to film. I just hope that when people saw the film, they could see why we made it.

Covid and the policies around it have become a divisive, political issue. If you'd been to that hospital, seen those people risking their lives day in day out, not just because it was their jobs but because it was the right thing to do, you'd never think there were two sides. It was a human issue.

Both Sides

I'm ambidextrous. I used to use both hands to write, equally messily as the teachers at school took pains to point out. Eventually I settled on writing with my left, though I do occasionally write with my right, but I play tennis with both hands. I fence with my left. I box southpaw and orthodox. I tend to do more dextrous things with my left and heavy lifting with my right. It definitely helped with dance and movement.

I don't know if that's impacted this feeling I've had that I never want to do just one thing. I didn't want to give up rugby when I was at drama school, in leg warmers and doing all sorts of dance and movement classes. I loved doing both and I wanted to continue doing both. And I think it made me a more rounded person. But it can be a curse as well as a gift. You get the mickey taken out of you by the dancers *and* the rugby players.

I always try to see both sides when we're making a film (and as much as I can, in life). I don't want to go in with a story that I write in London, and then find the people to tell that story. I'd much rather get there with a rough area of interest and let the story come from what we document. The very best moments in making films are the extent to which something you knew was interesting is even more interesting than you thought. I've had interviews (including quite recently) where the journalist has clearly decided what the story was going

95

to be before they'd even met me, which didn't actually have much to do with me. But then written the story anyway. I don't believe in doing that, because all you end up doing is repeating the same stories you already know, not the stories you don't. It's the opposite of what my team and I try and do and a style of journalism that feels archaic and is hopefully heading for extinction. The problem is that lots of people don't want to admit they don't know things.

It can be tricky, when you try and balance up the ethics of making a film that could be seen to be giving someone who you shouldn't platform, and indeed someone that many find abhorrent. But I believe you can make a film about someone whose views you might not personally agree with and remain objective. I still believe that people need to encounter ideas they don't agree with. So I've spoken to murderers, rapists, drug dealers, torturers, poachers. I want to take people to meet that extremity because it can teach us something important about the way we all live. I don't think it's my job to judge, but if the viewer wishes to, it's up to them.

There are times when I've failed to see both sides. I've never had much time for people traffickers or the Ku Klux Klan, and I've never met a Nazi I liked, especially when they're threatening to put me in a dog cage and throw me out of a seventh-storey window. And I didn't much take to the senior member of the Taliban who told me with absolute certainty, and in direct opposition to all of the other Afghans I had spoken to, that the people of Afghanistan don't want women's rights. But, generally, I try and approach each situation on its own terms. Sometimes, though, you just can't.

I was in Musa Qala in Afghanistan where there had been an attack and a family of Afghans had been hit by shrapnel and had come to the medics at the district centre. And the mainly male medics and doctor were trying to deal with injured women and children.* I'll always remember the girl with a lollipop in her mouth, silent, as the medics removed shards of metal from her back.

You never forget that silence when a kid is so badly hurt they're not crying. Another child had a long needle inserted into her chest to remove the pressure from the internal bleeding. They lifted one guy's dishdasha off and he was holding his insides in with two hands.†

There was a woman in a burqa who was quiet and we thought she was OK, but suddenly there's a huge amount of blood spreading across the floor, until most of it was covered. The male medic goes across to her and the guy with his guts hanging out stands up and shouts at the medic not to touch her. Because his faith won't allow it.

I believe in not judging other people without trying to understand the context of their lives. Now, as I look back, I can see that to him, seriously injured, his wife about to die, there was a soldier about to touch her and make her unclean. But in that moment, as a female medic rushed to her side who would eventually save her life, there were two things I realised; the first that this was a situation I found very hard to see both sides of, the other was that a faith this strong was going to be almost impossible to counter.

It felt a very long way from being an actor, that's for sure.

---

* Years later I gave a speech to the paras who had returned from Afghanistan after evacuating British nationals from Kabul, and the doctor from that hospital was there.

† At this moment our executive producer Matt Bennett had to pick up the camera because others couldn't. Without Matt, *Extreme World* would never have happened. Thank you Matt.

The Largest of the Rooms

'As you can see, this is the largest of the rooms . . .' I'll never forget those words. During my entire time at drama school, they were a cause of huge amounts of stress.

It was essentially an exercise designed to help you say lines and carry out complicated stage directions at the same time, while making sure it seemed spontaneous. It was a long speech where someone introduced the different rooms of a house, while making a variety of hot drinks and serving sandwiches and biscuits at the same time. They would ask us all to do it at a certain point, so you'd have to be ready to go with it. It was like Russian roulette. You would be learning lines for fifteen different things, but you always had to have this monologue ready to go. And if you made a mistake, Hilary would be there to put a grenade under you.

Hilary Wood was Senior Lecturer in Acting at Webber Douglas. A striking, ageless, blonde woman. She had these piercing blue eyes. She wore lots of jewellery. She smoked Dunhill Blue and had a topaz lighter and matching blue rings. All us students bounded around her like puppies, desperate for her approval.

When she was praising you, you felt ten feet high. But if she was unhappy, she could take you to pieces. Those blue eyes became the eye of Sauron. One student wore diamanté earrings for a part and Hilary considered this to be an attempt at upstaging. I was physically wincing by the end of her comments, but also trying to hide so she didn't notice me.

She would come in with two coffees. She was the only one who was allowed to smoke. She was one of the most engaging people I've ever met. You can't teach it. She just held your attention. She'd put her coffees down. She'd take a cigarette out. Tap the cigarette on the pack. Take the lighter out of her bag. Light the cigarette. We're all just staring at her.

'Now, Johnny.' And everyone who wasn't Johnny would breathe out with relief. Johnny would get calmly taken to pieces, slumping down into his chair.

'Right, Mandy. You can't dry. You're letting other people down.'

She instilled in us all this idea that we had to be professionals. This wasn't a vanity project about you getting applause. You were a professional. This was your job. It wasn't about you. It was about the company, the show and ultimately the audience who you owed your professionalism to. For several weeks we had to go to London Zoo and find an animal. Then come back and be that animal for an entire hour. Some of the group thought it would be clever to come back and be a sloth. But this was not Hilary's first rodeo and bawled them out.

I'd done my year of leg warmers and a headband at Southend Tech, so felt like I knew this world, but drama school was a whole other level. Webber Douglas didn't actually have room for the number of students. The drama school was cramped into some of the most expensive real estate in London. You couldn't enter stage right from the main stage, because stage right was the back of someone's living room. I dread to think what it must have been like to be sitting down to dinner and the fiftieth version of 'There Ain't Nothing Like a Dame' comes blasting through your wall. So we would run from church hall to church hall having our classes. I learned Commedia dell'arte in St Mary's church hall, trying to avoid the rich-toddler sick of the playgroup that had it before us.*

It was like an entirely different language. One tutor was this wonderful enormous guy in his sixties, who'd worked with 'all the greats back in the day'. He wore a furry Russian hat, even on the hottest day of summer. He'd been in all these war movies in the fifties. He always had an unfiltered cigarette between his fingers, or was taking one out of his cigarette case, or was lighting one. He had this great rich deep husky voice, like a bag of gravel soaked in honey, all jowls, bald with hair coming out of his ears. He always wore a suit and tie. He would describe getting home at the end of a long day to us: 'I get home, feet up. Two fingers of whisky. Wonderful.'

He'd take you through your performance saying, 'Act one. Act one you were a bit bangers and mash. That's fine. But Act 2, we need to make an omelette.'

I smiled and nodded. Then sometimes, he'd say I was 'a bit porridgey'.

I assumed it meant something about the level of finesse in the performance but I'm still not absolutely sure.

There were plenty of people who came from wealth there. But students from all sorts of backgrounds too. It might have been hard to get a grant, but grants meant that you got people from all sorts of backgrounds. The only thing that was slightly galling was that there were lots of people who had very wealthy self-employed parents who didn't declare tax. Meanwhile, there was me with my dad, employed by the government, who had to.

---

* This was in the centre of the Boltons, one of the most desirable areas of West London, where houses now go for around £32 million.

For one exercise early on, we had to pretend to be ourselves in twenty years' time. 'I'm Ross Kemp, I sell cars for a living in Essex.'*

Over the next few years, alongside classes, I cleaned pub toilets, I was a terrible bouncer and a slightly better waiter than I'd been at the golf club.† I'm not sure what the other blokes on the course thought of me, or where to put me. There were three guys who came from similar backgrounds who formed a bit of a clique. They would be there whispering, critiquing other people's performances. At one point they decided it would be funny to say I was smelly. I couldn't be entirely sure it was just cattiness. There was one shower for about a hundred people. And we were constantly exercising. You'd go from a two-hour dance class to a two-hour movement class to a mime course. And I was off at the weekend playing rugby. I'd come back with 'welcome to Wales' tattooed on my back with studs and too stiff to do a plié.

Meanwhile, when I went back to Essex, all my mates in the pub would be horrified at my new RP voice. 'Why you talking like that, Ross?'

Some people just didn't get on with it. I had a mate who left at the end of our second year. And plenty of other people left along the way too.

There were a *lot* of Stanislavski techniques, including Hilary's speciality: the three circles of concentration.‡

---

* In many ways I did go into sales. Just not cars, but me.
† Back then, I'd panicked that a lady at the table I was serving was having a heart attack or a stroke but it turned out I'd just accidentally tipped an ice-cold bottle of tonic water down the back of her dress.
† Basically, a whole lot of techniques invented by a famous Russian man for creating believable characters and helping actors inhabit them fully.

101

'There are three circles of concentration and I'm going to show you what first circle is.' Hilary draws a chalk circle around herself. And I'm half wondering if she's going to get candles and a goat's skull out and do some witchcraft.

She glares out at a room full of bemused first-year drama students. 'First circle.' She snaps to attention. 'I am talking to the self. I am exploring my thoughts and feelings, but I am channelling inwards.'

'Second Circle.' She fixes us with a look and draws another circle that intersects with the first circle and pulls a student into it, speaking more loudly. 'I am in conversation with other actors around me. My energy is drawing those on stage in towards me.'

'And third circle.' She gets us all to stand up and go outside and she points to a spire in Putney and shouts, 'I am engaging THE WHOLE WORLD with my energy.'

It was a very different time. We had one movement teacher who would pace around like a cat. She taught us that you had to understand your body and be comfortable with it. The way she did this was mainly by feeling bits of your body. In one movement class, I remember her steering me around by my buttocks.

We put on an awful production of *Twelfth Night*. It was a minimalist set, non-historical costumes. Just a simple rostrum. Bamboo canes for swords. And we were wearing these things called 'jazz bells'. They were a kind of woollen flared trousers. Itchy wool. I'm glad that these seem to have disappeared. And jazz shoes, which are like a ballet shoe but with laces and a small heel. And black T-shirts (those have endured). That was drama school. Jazz shoes and jazz bells from French's in Leicester Square. And there I am playing Antonio in *Twelfth Night*. I've always enjoyed Shakespeare, though I don't think I'm particularly good at it.

We got to the end and the only sound you could hear was the sound of the chairs flipping back up as people quietly left. Backstage we lined up for a curtain call, before the stage manager in a very deadpan way said, 'You need an audience for a curtain call.'

At the end of term, they would make us all perform two songs in front of the whole school. They thought it was important to perform in front of your peers. There is no more vicious critic than your peer group. And everyone would turn up, to witness the car crashes. It could be completely inhumane. Years later, I would watch things like *The X Factor* with an awful pang of recognition.

Someone I knew absolutely lost it and couldn't sing. She just stood on stage, weeping in front of the entire school, trying to sing 'Bring on the Clowns'. The tears came to her eyes and her right leg was twitching like she was being electrocuted. 'Bring on . . . the cloooooooowns.' I still feel their pain.

I always chose big Rodgers and Hammerstein numbers like 'Oh What a Beautiful Morning' so I could belt them out. At least there was a good chance the audience would know and like the song. Singing makes you very vulnerable. I'd try and sing songs in character, so I had something to shelter behind. Some people just went out there and relied on their singing technique. That would have felt utterly terrifying.

I felt like some of the tutors took it too far at times. Some of them hadn't had the career they wanted and didn't get regular work and were a little crueller than they needed to be. I remember one of them turned to one of our group and said, 'You're a good-looking boy but you're not very engaging. I want you out of my rehearsal room.' And some of them were filling in there until their big break arrived, and they definitely took it out on those they taught. People would vent their frustrations with graffiti on the toilet walls. When I left I wrote, *Don't stamp on the daffodils.*

Ultimately though, they were putting us through this to prepare us for the professional world of performing. They wanted us to be rounded and have all the potential skills to deal with an industry that just didn't take any prisoners. When I look back, it was good training for turning up in some of the situations I've found myself in when making the documentaries.*

But it could be extremely hard on your ego.

---

* Men with guns hold no fear when you've had a bitchy twenty-year-old drama student stage-whispering a critique of your Antonio.

The Ego Has Landed

I definitely struggled with ego at points in my life. I think perhaps it started with some of my experiences at school, where I developed this shell as a defence. Then, going into drama school and being an actor, it's just such a subjective business. Walking into an audition where they take one look at you, or hear you say one line and just say 'no, thank you'. Or they make you say the lines in so many different ways and you never find out why what you did was wrong. As much as you're playing a part, saying someone else's words, when you're an actor, the product is essentially you. That's great when it's the applause and the acclaim because it's for you. But anything negative and it's not so great. So you either develop a way to cope with it, or it drives you round the bend. You have to have a defence mechanism to deal with the rejection. And then when things start going a bit better for you, if you've still got that shell, then it can harden into a kind of ego. That was definitely me for a period when I was young.

Wherever it came from, I've certainly been guilty of putting myself at the centre of the universe, especially at the height of fame, which now feels ridiculous. I'm sure there are people out there who bear grudges against me, some of them justified. Because I was immature and selfish and generally a bit of a twit.

There are women who I knew when I was younger, especially, who I wish I could apologise to, because I know I didn't treat them the way they deserved to be treated. I found it hard to look past my own short-term interests and happiness and sometimes that meant relationships ended in not particularly kind ways. If I met the younger me now, I'd be tempted to take him into a corner and give him some very strong life advice. This idea of toxic masculinity that exists out there at the moment, festering online, which equates being a strong man with disrespecting and denigrating women, I have no time for that at all. I don't recognise that 'strength'. It's the opposite of everything I believe and was taught.

All I can say is that some of my bad choices have hurt me at least as badly as anyone else. When we think about our own bad choices we know the context, all the factors, what was going on in our lives and we know how we feel about them now. But when it's someone else's behaviour, there's the temptation to say, 'Well they did that because they're a bad person.' Life is rarely that simple.

I think that's something that both drama *and* documentaries can do if they're good – they can take you inside other people's lives and show you what shaped them and their choices.

I don't think I properly grew up until I went to Afghanistan. Those trips were, literally, a hard slap in the face.

I developed quite a sweety habit while I was out there. Partly it was just something to do. Something to look forward to, a reward for getting to the next compound. My favourite was a famous brand of square fruit-flavoured chewy sweets. Perhaps it was also that the sugar took me back to my childhood. But when you were doing twelve-hour patrols and you weren't allowed to speak, the next sweet became a massive morale booster.*

---

* I also had my Grandad Kemp on my shoulder who would talk to me. He was my guardian angel.

We used to hand out sweets to kids in Afghanistan. I and a brilliant soldier called Stevie Ray used to do it. What could be more universal than giving sweets to kids? Winning hearts and creating cavities.

One day, I was on a patrol going through the green zone. People associate the fighting in Afghanistan with the desert, but often you're fighting over the poppy fields, because that's the land that the Taliban want to control. Because then they control the money. So you're often fighting in irrigated land. This was where you'd get the really close-up fighting. You knew the Taliban were near, when the order came down the line to 'fix bayonets'. Particularly when you didn't have one, or anything to fix it to. It's tempting to imagine that technology has transformed warfare, but that's the same order that's been coming down the line for more than three hundred years. You never forget the cascading metal clink of fifty odd bayonets being attached to SA80 rifles. When it comes down to it, it's about men on the ground with sharp things.

I remember we were on patrol once and I saw this kid. And you had to be careful as often they were dickers (lookouts), watching out for the troops and then they'd tell the enemy where you were. A lot of the time, the Taliban dickers would be on little 50cc motorbikes. Sometimes they were kids. Sometimes they'd be in the fields, dressed as farmers and then they'd stand up with a gun. So I see this kid and he's driving goats down the path with what looks like a long aerial snapped off something. I'm just opening a packet of fruity chewy sweets, and I offer him one. And he takes the sweet with one hand and hits me straight across the face with the car aerial with the other. This wasn't the reaction I'd been expecting.

The local religious leaders had got wise to the fact that sweets were being handed out. And they'd worked out that these sweets have gelatine in, which sometimes comes from pigs, so it's haram. The welt across my face was there for two weeks, a reminder that you might think you know the way the world works. But you don't.

I certainly didn't hand out any more sweets after that.

I'd begun the process of growing up before Afghanistan, when I was making those first documentary films about gangs. Becoming a father helps. As does getting a bit of perspective on what actually matters, what actually makes you happy. For the first thirty-odd years, you're essentially just working out the basics of being a person. A lot of people can trip through life never thinking about much. But it's always been in my nature to lift rocks, even when sometimes I haven't much liked what was underneath.

Being a parent is also a reminder that you're not in control of the most important things in life. You can try your hardest to give your kids the best start, to make them feel loved and supported. But in the end, they've got to live their life, you can't do it for them. And you can try and make sure you do the best job you can, remember what it felt like to be a child and fix any mistakes when it's your turn. But they'll still end up rolling their eyes at you. It's part of the cycle of life.

There's also that balance between trying to give them a better life than you had, that fundamental parental impulse, and getting them to appreciate how lucky they are to have what they have.* How lucky we all are. I remember coming

---

* I am appalled to find myself now using phrases my dad used to use with me like, 'You don't know how easy you have it', but I suppose that's the natural consequence of striving for a better life for them. They *will* have it easier. That's the whole point.

back from a trip to Syria, where I'd met a five-year-old boy who was surviving by stripping the watches and jewellery from corpses. He could not only count, he could work out the value of gold in multiple currencies. I came home to my five-year-old who was disappointed I hadn't been able to bring him a present back from the airport. I had to remind myself that it wasn't his fault he didn't know about this other kid's life. He shouldn't. No one should. At their age, they should be focusing on *Paw Patrol*.*

---

* When you've got young kids, you end up watching a lot of children's television. And, often, you're quite out of it with tiredness because you've got young kids. And you slip into a kind of trance watching it. That happened for me with *Paw Patrol*, which I wish I'd invented. Leaving aside the fact that these are talking dogs who can drive, you start thinking thoughts like: Does every city have their own Paw Patrol? Is the kid, Ryder, paying a living wage to the dogs? And the police dog is also a spy dog, which feels dangerously close to the Adventure Bay secret police. I've been all around the world and I can tell you that level of connection between the judiciary and the security forces never goes well for the population.

Also, the rules are that dogs can talk? But cats and chickens can't? But we know cats can understand English because the mayor of the next town has a group of cats who can understand his instructions. And why is there no specific medical pup, but instead medicine is part of the many responsibilities of the Scottish (because the highlands) mountain rescue dog? Where does the fire dog Marshall's infinite supply of water come from? And they're an emergency service but they get pulled into all sorts of other stuff – helping local restaurants and farmers, organising parties. I would have serious worries about the wide remit the Patrol are asked to fulfil impacting their ability to do their actual job. Or is that just me?

The Glue Kids

I'm doing an interview while, in the background, a young pregnant girl is nursing a baby. She has one of these glue bottles in her mouth and is inhaling. Then she takes the bottle and gives it to the baby. Then puts it in her own mouth. As I watch, the baby starts crying and she gives the bottle back to it. And it stops crying. I've never seen anything like it.

I was forty-three years old, and we were in Kenya for *Gangs* to make a film about the Mungiki, a gang who had been labelled the most dangerous in the whole of Africa. They were reported to cut people's heads off and skin their skulls. Cut them up and leave them in different places. I went and met three of the top members just outside of Nairobi. All of them were wearing pinstriped suits. Their founder was in prison for possession of drugs and guns. We knew they'd spotted us on our way into the meeting point and as we stood in this gutted room, waiting, feeling very exposed in the middle of nowhere, time passed very slowly.

They told me that their violent reputation was government propaganda.* It was difficult to discern who was telling the

---

* Four weeks after we'd left, two of the men were shot by government forces.

At one point I was inducted into the Mungiki. You have to be on Mount Kenya at first light and, as part of the process, they dip this special brush truth. But what was absolutely true was that the huge upsurge in tribal violence had created an enormous number of orphans and displaced children.

About a hundred of these children had congregated on this rubbish tip, picking through what has been thrown away to find food. The smell of rotting rubbish and smoke filled the air. There were children huddled around fires. They had these small plastic bottles, and they'd stir the contents with a stick and huff the fumes. We learned that this was glue. And the 'glue' isn't a street name for a drug. It's a thick industrial glue made from boiling down animal bones and used for upholstery and shoe repair. Users inhale it, normally out of old plastic water bottles, and it gives an intense high. It's highly addictive and very poisonous.

The ethics of making films in the sort of places that we have done is a constant battle. The simple fact that you're dropping into places that are often impacted by extreme poverty and you could make a difference. Whether it's giving what you've got in your wallet or putting across their point of view to the wider world, you are impacting everyone you film. The team and I think about that a lot. My position is that I try and minimise our impact. Yes, we're there, and yes, we're asking questions and filming, but my reasoning is that I don't know enough about the context on the ground to take action. If I change the situation then I'm not documenting it, I'm shaping it. The fixers that we work with can sometimes be putting their lives in danger by working with us. You've got to be so careful with your impact. But we had to step in this time.

---

thing made from animal hair in a mixture of oil and something pungent. And then they whack you in the face with it. The whole process is finished off by eating sandwiches and drinking milky tea.

We spoke to boys who told us they took the glue to forget the things they had seen. We saw addicts, foaming at the mouth and shaking. One boy told us about the long-term effects of glue on him and that he constantly heard voices and just wanted to rest. They told us of seeing their parents cut down in front of them. Of losing their entire families. Some of them were lured into petty crime. They weren't safe. They were the targets of constant violence. The police were their worst enemies, beating them.

We met the former street boys who had begun running programmes for the children on rubbish dumps. Who stood in as their family. We spoke to children about how those charities looked after them, bought them clothes, talked to them, to change their lives. To see how little made such a huge difference, it was heartbreaking. The charity workers there told me that everything a child needed to go to school was £35. For less than £3 they could provide three meals a day for a child. All those kids wanted were books and uniforms to go to school.

One boy said that he used to feel jealous that other children were able to enjoy themselves when he could not. But then he realised that was just the way it is. He was nine years old.

I think often of the footage of ex street children, receiving their first school uniforms, their smiles and laughter. I feel proud that after donations following the film we made, two boys were reunited with their families. There are some things in my life I'm not proud of. But I'm proud of that.

All Mod Cons

I lived in a variety of places during drama school, including, at one point, with my then girlfriend in the pub around the corner from drama school. But before that I lived with my friend Joe Williams. Joe was six foot with the natural grace of a dancer. He had a voice like rolled gold. He sounded like Orson Welles despite being from a very tough part of Leeds. From time to time he wore an afro and loved to surprise pub landlords when he ordered, as they really weren't expecting that voice to come out of him.

One day he said to me he'd found a room for us in South Kensington, a five-minute walk from drama school, just off the Old Brompton Road. Forty-five quid a week, that's £22.50 each. Sold.

So we arrived at the address, 17 Cranley Gardens, me with my obligatory Greenfield rucksack full of cans of sausage, beans, tuna and cornflakes, which was pretty much the entirety of our diet at that point.* We used to make a massive bowl of tinned tuna, cornflakes and mayonnaise and eat it

---

* While we lived there, my mother got a call from my grandmother, who was under the impression we were living three doors down from the other Cranley Gardens in Muswell Hill, which became briefly very famous in 1983 as the address where serial killer Dennis Nilsen was arrested. It had come out that he was murdering and eating young boys. My grandmother was quite alarmed when the news first broke.

cold with a little bit of chilli sauce. It would fill you up, and it could last a week in the fridge.

At first sight, 17 Cranley Gardens had this grand-looking entrance, but the stucco had come unstuck and the white pillars were peeling. When you came in the entire hallways smelled of this pungent sweet, sour, earthy smell, which I later found out was borscht.

That was back in the early eighties, when South Kensington had a large Eastern European population. Lots of Arab families, lots of Lebanese but mainly Eastern European. Our drama school tutors were all obsessed with 'the Russians' too, who they told us had invented modern acting via the Stanislavski technique.

It was about six floors high and we're going up all these flights of stairs. We kept on going up flight after flight, until we came to a floor where panes of glass were missing in the windows, just these wrecked net curtains billowing where there was no glass. And my feet started to stick to the floor. That was the first moment I wasn't sure if I wanted to stay here. There were four doors on that top landing. As soon as I opened the door to our room, all I could smell was urine. I went to open the window directly opposite, but it had been nailed shut. As I looked out, I remember seeing the lightbulbs on Harrods and thinking this was a very long way from anything Harrods had to offer.*

The wallpaper had once been eggshell blue, but it was coming off the wall where the plaster was sagging with damp. There was a Formica fake marble table covered in cigarette burns on a chrome base that wobbled. There were two chairs,

---

* Little did I know that twenty years later I would go to Harrods on a regular basis, but back then it may as well have been Mars.

a brown rug and a fake marble column balanced in one corner. In another corner there was a sink with a cracked mirror above it and a Belling freestanding stove with the Bakelite knobs all broken off. Next to that was a cupboard with the door coming off. There were two beds. There was a filled-in fireplace. There was a Chinese dresser that had been screwed shut. And there was a fridge full of mildew. That was it.

The beds were pushed together, so we separated them. I put binbags down on my one, then my sleeping bag on top, because the mattress didn't look like something I wanted against my skin

Now my mate Joe came from Chapeltown, a pretty tough area in Leeds, and he was certainly more streetwise than me. He'd lived all around the world. We decided we had to stay at least one night, so we sat at the wobbly table and ate some beans with sausages and/or some cornflakes. We were sitting there talking, when out of the corner of my eye, I saw one end of the carpet slowly rise up. It was one of those carpets that was probably maroon at some point but was now just carpet-coloured. But it was floating. So I said, 'Did you see that?' We just sat there, frozen.

And then it happened again. And the smell of urine got even stronger. We worked out that what was happening was that there were such large gaps between the floorboards that every time someone opened a door or a window downstairs, the air was blowing up into our flat and lifting the edges of the carpet.

So Joe's asleep on the other side of room, crashed out. And I'm lying there thinking, if this is what it takes, I don't want to be an actor. I hate acting. I want to be on TV but I'm never going to, because I can't do this. All of a sudden, this light comes on in the corner of the room like something out of *Close Encounters* and I call out, 'Joe. *What* is that?' But he doesn't make a noise. It's on me.

I'm in my pants in my sleeping bag and I get up and put my trainers on because I don't want to tread on the sticky floor, and I'm trying to work out how there's light coming from under the sink.* So I shuffle quietly and I can see there's a cupboard door under the stove and the light is coming out of it. I turn back to Joe, but he's still out of it. I very slowly open the door underneath the stove. And the light gets brighter. I don't want to put my knees on the carpet, so instead I bend down and look into the cupboard and that's when I see the back of a pair of ankles, with a large pair of very bright pink knickers down around them.

The next morning we work out that the shared toilet for all three rooms was behind that cupboard, and anything that missed the bowl came flowing under the cooker, straight into our room.

We stayed in that room for over a year. It was such a short walk to drama school. But I'll never forget those bright pink knickers.

---

* My bare feet have subsequently encountered far smellier and stickier things than that floor.

Libya

'Open the drawer, Ross.' Something about the way my friend and director, Marta Shaw, says it gets my attention. I open it and inside are pairs and pairs of large, pink frilly knickers. I lift a pair up by my finger. 'Not sure they'll fit me.'

'No, underneath the knickers,' she whispers. I pull them back and there, underneath, are about twelve Mills grenades. Think of the most cartoon grenade you can. Then pull the pin out of the pineapple one. Those. Nervously I open the next drawer. Bras this time, big ones, and underneath them, four RPG warheads. I very gently put the underwear back and look at Marta. It's always dangerous to rifle through another man's wife's underwear drawer. But it felt especially so this time.

It's 2016 and we're in Libya to make a film about refugees coming from sub-Saharan Africa to get to Europe. It's the deadliest migrant route in the world. A thousand miles of desert then the sea crossing from Tripoli to Italy. At the time, three thousand people a week are making the journey and twelve people a day are dying. Women would take birth control when attempting it because of the extreme likelihood of being raped – there was a 90 per cent chance of it happening. It is a truly horrific journey. But it is still better than what they are coming from. Anyone who thinks it's too easy hasn't seen that route. We're the first Westerners, and only journalists, to make it there in a long time.

We're staying at a trafficker's house in the middle of the desert, arranged by our fixer. He just won't stop showing us his AK-47. He's slightly balding but he's constantly preening his hair like Elvis. Chain-smoking in his green uniform and matching baseball cap. He absolutely loves himself. His wife and kids aren't there. Me and the crew are all staying in different configurations in different rooms and it's me and my mate soundman Dave in together.

We've already seen the patrols stopping the boats piled high out of Tripoli, seen a suspected people trafficker being dragged naked over cobblestones till he looked like a piece of meat.

We've driven along the land route, watching as trucks and cars laden down with people made their way through the vicious heat. Nothing but endless brown sand everywhere you look.

There would be 100-metre queues at petrol stations in one of the most oil-rich countries in the world. They would watch us.

At one point I see smoke from tyres burning on the horizon and realise that's where we're heading. We get to the smoke and the trafficker gets out of the car to talk to the crowd and starts to argue. And it turns out they're there because of us. To protest about the West destroying their country.[*]

He's trying to explain that we're there to tell the story of the people being trafficked but also why trafficking people has become one of the few things that people can do. But the voices are raised and the gestures are becoming more wild. We're pulled up tight behind a Land Cruiser. And then another one pulls up right behind us and we're hemmed in. I don't like this. One of the first things they teach you on your courses about hostile environments is never to get hemmed in. 'Ah shit, we're going to get taken here.'

------

[*] Which to be honest was a fair point.

I jump into the driver's seat, ready to start the engine and try to drive away if we need to. I don't know where I thought I'd go – we're hundreds of miles from Tripoli and I have no idea how to get there – I just want to try and show we're not going to be easy to kidnap. The crowd seems to be getting angrier and angrier. I've got about a foot and a half in front and foot and a half behind, so I start to reverse back and then go forward and I get the car out, but there's a knock on the window and there's guns. And the people trafficker is waving his finger and looking very unhappy. I tell him I just want to get away from the angry mob setting things on fire. So we get back to the flat. And the translator is saying the villagers are very upset that you're here and you need to go. But there's only one flight a week.

And then suddenly word comes back that we have to go to our different rooms and stay there. And there are lots more people we've never seen before coming in and out of the flat, all carrying different weapons. So there's me and Dave on our own. Marta, Mark* and Jamie in another room. And every time we put our head out into the corridor there's a man with a gun who shakes his head. Our phones are taken away (but not Dave's iPod, which I am about to regret) and the door is shut. You don't have to be a member of MI6 to know that we're in danger.

Dave decides that now is the perfect time to begin my education in the German techno pop and in particular the music of Kraftwerk. In an airless room, as we wait to find out what's going to happen to us.

'We drive, drive, drive on the autobahn . . .' Dave is a soundman. Dave can tell you in lots of detail why a particular

---

* Thanks Mark McCauley, the coolest cameraman I've ever worked with.

moment in a song is especially interesting. For twelve hours. If that doesn't fit the definition of cruel and unusual punishment, I don't know what does. Whatever was going to happen to us, I did not want that to be the last thing going through my head. As I lay there, contemplating a very uncertain future, unable to get Kraftwerk out of my head, I turn to Dave.

'Dave?'

'Yeah.'

'If they do shoot us tomorrow, I hope they shoot you first.'

There was a stressful night with not much sleep. But the next morning, we weren't shot. Instead, we were bundled into cars and taken to an airfield and got a plane to Tripoli and from there to a safe house. I would later be told by trusted UK sources that there had been a credible attempt to kidnap us, in particular Marta.

Where Not to Get Kidnapped

'Have we been taken?' I look at our fixer and he is staring straight ahead, his face worryingly pale. 'Yes, I think so.'

Of all the places not to be kidnapped, Nigeria is near the top of my list. I was forty-four years old, and we had spent time in Lagos and then a place called Port Harcourt trying to interview a group called the Movement for the Emancipation of the Niger Delta, or MEND. They called themselves activists. The government called them kidnappers and pirates. The exact balance between their cause and their status as a criminal organisation was never clear to me. The reason for this conflict was oil.*

There is a huge amount of oil in Nigeria. They're the biggest producer of oil in Africa but they have very little capacity to refine it themselves, which weirdly means they export huge amounts of oil but import petrol. The imbalance between those

---

* The corruption and bureaucracy I saw in Nigeria was like nothing I have ever seen. Going about our day-to-day business, we were regularly asked, 'Do you have something for the weekend?' – which was an invitation to bribe them. I was at the airport in Port Harcourt trying to get out, with my luggage halfway through the X-ray machine, and it just stopped. I looked at the woman running it and she said, 'Perhaps you have something for the weekend?' I shook my head and reached my hand in. She said, 'Put your hand in there again and I'll chop it off.' So I just pointed at the director and said, 'He's the bossman.' I looked forward to her conversation with a very tough, Scottish director about getting blood out of a stone.

with wealth and those without is stark around the world and getting wider, but in Nigeria at this time it felt particularly apparent and exacerbated by corruption.

We had been to meet the governor of one of the states in the Niger Delta, who had white Versace tables with gold inlay. He made me wait three hours for him. Then fed me a chilli jam doughnut and then was very amused with the face I pulled.* There were a huge number of cars on the road. He had a car behind him with an old Russian heavy machine gun, which they would fire over the traffic to clear it. Just to be around him was utterly surreal.

Then we travelled out to see the impact of oil on the environment.

What happened was that oil companies would put in these test wellheads to see if there was enough oil for it to be worth their time to drill properly. But if there wasn't, they'd just leave the wellheads, which were capped off but people would come along and uncap them to get to the oil, which would leak into the surrounding areas. Or they'd put in pipelines, which would crack. Often, instead of going by pipeline, the companies would use smaller tankers that would come in, top up from the wellheads sticking up out of the mud, and then sail out to the super-tankers and offload the oil to them. And MEND would do this too. Stealing oil and selling it on to the super-tankers.

Oil is toxic stuff. It burns your skin if it gets on you. If oil gets into the water, it poisons the plants and it poisons the animals. We went to a fractured pipeline where the oil had poisoned the mangroves for miles around, and they looked like dead white fingers.

---

* One of the many governors at this time managed to escape the authorities dressed as a woman with millions of dollars in his bags.

We were heading out to meet the Ogoni people whose way of life as fishermen had been destroyed by the pollution from the oil. There are abandoned oil tankers along the banks. The Ogoni took the lifeboats from these abandoned tankers to use. They want to take us to a pipeline break, to show us the environmental devastation that leads to. I'm in a T-shirt, military boots and jungle trousers. Our fixer, who is a journalist, is wearing a Marks and Spencer pinstripe suit and black brogues. It's hotter than hell. Overcast and I'm already sweating buckets. I have no idea how he's going to last in a heavy suit.

As I always do, before we went out to Nigeria, I'd looked at the risk assessment and what came up was the frequency of rape of the oil workers who were kidnapped. And at one point it said something like, 'If you're taken, there is an 80 per cent chance of rape and a 40 per cent chance of rape with a penis.' I had never thought about that before, but I was about to.

After forty minutes or so, we jump off the boat into the mangrove swamp. We should be in the middle of a green, vibrant landscape. But it's dead. The air is choked with fumes. Everything is dead. Your eyes are stinging so you can't see 50 metres away from the source of the oil, it's that toxic.* My mate in the Marks and Spencer suit is suffering dreadfully. From the waist up, he's business casual, from the waist down he's swamp monster. We're wading along, getting footage of the devastation as they explain how much of the region is like this. How the old way of fishing and harvesting periwinkles are gone.

The director, Euan, the cameraman, Will, and the soundman, Kiff, are in one boat. Then there's me and the guy in the Marks

_____

* I don't know about his brogues but by the time I'd got home from that trip, my jungle boots had melted.

123

and Spencer suit in the other boat with about ten members of the Ogoni. By this point he's clearly not very happy because his trousers are pretty much covered in oil and mangrove mud. We're tired and sweating and just desperate for a glass of water. And we're going at a rate of knots, fast enough for the light rain to start stinging our faces. The other boat is about 50 metres ahead of us, filming us as we make our way back.

And then, all of a sudden, our boat is peeling off to the right and the other boat is carrying straight on.

And I immediately assume this is it. We've been taken. And now there's a very good chance that something not very nice is going to happen to us. I turn to the suit guy and he's looking extremely worried. And that's when I say, 'Have we been taken?' And he just stares straight ahead and says, 'Yes, I think so.'

It's one of the few times in my life where I've been reminded that the phrase 'your heart sinks' is true. It really did feel as if my heart was sinking down through my chest to my stomach. We'd spoken to people who'd been kidnapped and they were not easy stories to listen to.

Then I look around the boat and I'm starting to wonder who's part of the kidnap, and who's a victim and what order whatever happens next is going to happen in. And that's a very strange thing to start thinking about. I could see my friend in the ruined suit was thinking exactly the same thing. We're in that boat for another fifteen minutes, which is an extremely long time when that's going through your head. We come around the corner and come back to the village and I have never been so relieved in my life. Rather squeakily, I ask the guy why we'd gone a different route to the other boat and that's when he says, 'We wanted to beat them back here, for a joke.'

And I very weakly smile. 'What an excellent joke.'

Smoke and Mirrors

'Is this some sort of joke?' Joe had handed me the phone because the emergency service operator won't believe it's not a prank.

Somehow we'd ended up in Joe's older brother's flat. We were on the North Peckham Rise estate that was notorious for being one of the roughest in London.* It was one of those cheap, mass-produced estates built in the sixties and seventies. By the time we went to live on it, it was falling apart. Someone must have gotten rich, because they didn't spend the money on the estate. Everything was falling apart, or stained, or rotting or all three. The lifts were permanently out of order.

The whole thing was like a labyrinth of tunnels and alleyways going from the outer ring into the inner rings. And at the centre of the circle was a massive rubbish bin. If you can find a better metaphor for how the powers that be thought of the people that lived in this sort of housing you'd have to work pretty hard. Every night I ran from the bus stop to the flat to avoid the bored guys who would sporadically decide to chase you.

The lighting never worked, which meant you were incredibly vulnerable as you moved around the estate too. The inner

---

* It was already pretty notorious by the time we lived there and subsequently demolished.

bit was where the older residents tended to live. And that's where our flat was, in Saul Court, on the third floor.

It always seemed to be forty degrees and you couldn't open any windows, so it was great in winter, not so good in summer. There were no carpets. I slept on a mattress that I had wedged into my then girlfriend's car and driven over. I put a sleeping bag on it. Joe had the bedroom with an actual bed in it. You had to go through my room to get to the kitchen, which looked inwards into the estate.

It was all plastic tiles. There was a small room in the flat that Joe's brother had been very clear that we weren't to go into because that's where he ran his import and export business. It was all very Trotter Independent Traders. And he'd taken the dial off the telephone, so we couldn't go racking up any phone bills.

We were still at drama school, but a bowl of cornflakes, tuna and mayonnaise could last a week.

One night, I opened the door to take my girlfriend to her car and it was like dry ice, there was smoke all along the floor of the corridor. It was like the *Top of the Pops* studio. But it wasn't a smoke effect, it was actual smoke. I saw the smoke was wafting out of the rubbish chutes. So I sent her back to the flat and followed it along for a bit and got to the centre, where it turned out someone – kids, I assumed – had started a fire in the massive bin in the centre of our court. It must have been around 5 November. And I'm just watching as this smoke is going under the doors of the flats in the innermost ring of the estate, which is where the older people are. And there's all sorts in that bin – plastic, nappies, a mattress, it's not particularly nice smoke (not that any smoke ever is). And I was worried the old people were going to suffocate.

Of course, this is before mobile phones. So I get Joe out of bed from where he is with his girlfriend and we work out there's no point trying the phone boxes nearest to the estate as they're always broken. Joe says we'll have to use the phone. But I point out that the dial has been taken off. And it turns out Joe knows a magic trick. It turns out if you tap the cradle of the phone nine times, that's one nine dialled. If you do that three times, you can call the fire brigade.

So there's Joe with his remarkable molten-gold voice: 'Hello my good man, we're on Saul Court in Peckham. I wonder if you could send several fire engines as there's quite a blaze.' And that's when I had to take the phone and confirm that no, this wasn't a prank, and yes, we genuinely did need a fire engine quite urgently.*

It's odd when I look back at this stage in my life, because even though we didn't have money for food, even though we lived in an estate that was falling to bits and now on fire, even though we spent every day running the gauntlet of our drama teachers and fellow students, and all the evidence pointed to the contrary, I had this unshakeable belief that one day I was going to be on the telly.

---

* Joe left before the end of the final year. He'd had enough of drama school. I would stay with him for the night in Leeds when I went up for my final audition for *Emmerdale Farm*. Then we lost touch until they did *This Is Your Life* while I was in *EastEnders* and I heard that incredible rolled gold voice again.

On the Telly

'Make sure to ask him about his toes,' says the journalist.

'His toes?!'

'Just trust me.'

We were in Glasgow (one of my favourite cities), making a film about whether the welfare system was fit for purpose in the modern world. We met a couple who were living under a bridge, both heroin addicts. She paid for the drugs by selling herself.

Next we met Neil, a forty-six-year-old alcoholic who'd had three heart attacks and suffered from cirrhosis of the liver. Neil had had a hard life. You'd believe he was twenty years older than he was from looking at his face. He had painted the Samaritans' phone number in massive numbers on his front room wall. We went into his kitchen where he had one tin of £1 sausages in the cupboard. Every single pot in the kitchen was coated in crusted-on fat. The toilet floor and surface was covered in crystals of urine. He'd been in and out of prison most of his life. He was estranged from his wife and family. He could just about get down the stairs still, and once a week he'd go and get his benefits, place a bet and buy a few cans. He couldn't afford to pay for the heating, so it was colder inside the flat than it was outside. He was limping badly, so I asked the obvious question. He told me he'd pulled his toes off.

'Why did you do that?' I ask.

'The pain was so bad.'

'What did you do with them?'

And he replies in a very matter-of-fact way: 'Well, two of them's on top of the telly.' And then he limps over and picks up two brown, wrinkled objects and holds them out to me. 'That's the big toe and the wee toe, I think,' he says. 'There's another one lying around somewhere.'

Now they're closer, I can clearly see bone sticking out of one end and a nail at the other. He tells me that they'd lost circulation and were hurting so badly he'd got drunk one night and just wrenched them off. He didn't know what to do with them.

I can only look at him, astonished, with no idea what to say. 'That's probably not a good idea.'

Later, I asked him how he saw his future now, looking at where he was and his health and his reply was, 'I think, to the end of the year.' He spent his £75 a week on alcohol and the horses. He sat on his own. In his cold flat. No one ever came to see him.

We got quite a lot of complaints from people in Glasgow for that film. They felt we'd given an overly one-sided account of poverty, which gave the city a bad name and didn't make enough of the work they've done to improve people's lives. And it's certainly true that there are Neils in every city in Britain and it was nothing specific to Glasgow. But it's somewhere you can see the stark gap between rich and poor often within a couple of miles on the same street. We also met huge numbers of people doing everything humanly possible to alleviate poverty. I continue to think what I thought then: no one should have to live like that. There is something broken about revolving-door prisoners like Neil who have never worked, who are so addicted to alcohol they're killing themselves with it. It's a story I have heard all around the country again and again.

I have always had a real affinity with Glasgow. There's something about it that just feels like home. I think it was growing up in Essex, I feel at home in places that spend the whole week looking forward to the weekend. And Sauchiehall Street is the purest example of that. Years later Glasgow is where they shoot *Bridge of Lies*, and I love travelling up there and spending time in the city that I get and that gets me.

I was lucky enough to spend time in Afghanistan amongst some men from the Argyll and Sutherland regiment, who had been the thin red line at the Battle of Balaclava in the Crimean War, and they told me a story that made me cry with laughter.

A new commander comes in and he's very classic English. They're back in the UK after a tour and the RSM puts it to his commanding officer. 'Sir, some of the men and I would like to go on a religious pilgrimage. I think it would be very good for the lads – we have both Catholics and Protestants, as you know, and it would be a tremendous bonding opportunity.'

And this commanding officer is nodding along. 'Absolutely fabulous idea. Smashing. We're in Dover. Where are you thinking? Canterbury, perhaps?'

'No, sir, we're going to an abbey in Devon.'

The CO's a bit surprised but still enthusiastic. 'Smashing.'

And it transpires that the reason they're going to an abbey in Devon is because that is where the 'tonic wine' Buckfast is made. If you've never had it, Buckfast is made by adding pure caffeine to fortified wine. Basically a nineteenth-century vodka and Red Bull. Five days later, they were still trying to round them up. You had some people lost in Wales. You had some people who had decided to take up surfing in Cornwall.

There have been plenty of moments over the last twenty-five years where I've questioned what I'm doing, and holding another man's mummified toes was definitely one of those moments.

But that's just the way it is: things don't always happen in the order you want them to. Life isn't always a neat series of stepping stones.

Lies

'So, for your next stepping stone. Which of the following is a breed of dog? Dalmatian, or Siamese?' The woman hesitates. I assume she knows the answer. One of her team members is a third-year veterinary student. You don't back yourself on the category 'breeds of dog' over a trainee vet unless you know a lot about dogs. But she's hesitating. In the room backstage, the vet-to-be is jumping up and down. The contestant steps onto Siamese, which turns red with LIE. I have to be very careful to keep my face neutral as I commiserate with her. Should probably have let the future vet take that one.

It's 2022 and I am presenting a gameshow called *Bridge of Lies*. If you'd asked me when I was at drama school if I would ever do a gameshow, I'd have told you 'not for me'. I've been asked at various points over the years. There's not much I haven't been asked to do. When the script first arrived, I thought it was going to be for a drama. *Bridge of Lies*, it sounded like some sort of cold war spy thriller. But then when I started reading, as sometimes happens, I could just see it. I could see how it would work. It felt like that classic Saturday early evening family television I grew up with. And so, I found myself standing in front of a massive gantry in Glasgow.

I've always had a magpie brain, which squirrels away facts. Over the years, I've had to learn to very quickly absorb a huge amount about where we're about to film. My brain is full of the facts that remain from that process. I genuinely enjoy the process of seeing the things people know and don't know.

It's a game that gets played as a team, so I enjoy meeting people who are genuine friends.

And it's a nice change of pace for me to ask 'What do you do?' to someone and their answer not involve misery or desperation. We're not one of the shows that's giving away millions but even so, there was one woman who won and told me that the money meant she could buy Christmas presents for her grandchildren that year. (And yes, I did well up.)

There's plenty of times I look down at that bridge and think it's quite a nice analogy for my life. It was pretty straightforward for the first half. Then it got a bit trickier, and I started going sideways. But then I found my way across. I feel happy with where I've got to. I love my kids. I love my wife. I get to do a job I love.

Not bad for a boy from Essex.

Essex Boy

Essex has been especially visible over recent years because of the reality show. But those caricatures have been around for years. They were there when I was in *Birds of a Feather* with Sharon and Tracey, those archetypal Essex Girls. Essex Girls as an idea seems to have spread around the world as shorthand for all sorts of things, none of them particularly flattering. I wonder if it comes from Essex containing so many of those post-war new towns that sprung up and that idea of newness. When I was a teenager, in the eighties, there was a fascination with the gobby yuppy who went into the city and made money but had no class. People often couldn't understand why you'd want to go to drama school when you could go into the city and get yourself a Porsche Turbo. Get down to the Fontaine Bleau in Billericay for a Tequila Sunrise. Bosh.

And this was the era of dancing around your own handbags. But that Essex Girl joke bore no relationship to the girls that I met, who, while definitely interested in their appearance and having fun, were extremely sharp and clever.

The people I grew up with in Essex all seem to have been high achievers and I think there is a certain grafter quality that goes along with being from Essex. Not many of them went to university but they all own their own businesses and have done well financially in a massively diverse set of industries.*

There's lots of plumbers and carpenters and plasterers, lots of white vans parked in the front drive and people are snobby about that. There's a real working-class culture of being proud you've done well for yourself and showing it, whether that's a car, or clothes and jewellery or a night out. It became a place that symbolised white working-class culture and turned into a cartoon. And, of course, canny television producers took that cartoon and fed it back to viewers who expected that. But I've always been proud to be from Essex. I boxed and played rugby for my county. I'm sure there are grander places to be from but I'm very proud to be from there.

There's front but there's also incredible heart. I've always thought it's rooted in that English thing of the wrong 'sort' of money, which is just naked snobbery. It's a similar snobbery to the reaction I've got sometimes when I've been making films. It's been nearly twenty-five years since I was last in *EastEnders* regularly. I've made over 120 documentaries. But I still get the odd catty comments from journalists about 'Grant Mitchell' wanting to make a documentary. I think it comes from this idea that there's a journalism and media class. And if you're not from it, you need to keep your nose out. Well, I disagree with that. Why should we let the same narrow band of people decide which stories matter?

I don't mind that for myself. I made my peace with what happens when you play a role that lands as loudly as Grant Mitchell did a long time ago. For a big chunk of people, I am him. It doesn't matter what I do. And there are plenty of worse things you could be remembered for. But I think there's this

---

* Andy, Paul, Kanga, Steve M, Chesh, Duncan, Steve B – cheers to you all.

elitist attitude towards popularism and especially the 'wrong sort' of factual television. There's this idea that you should know things already and a whole type of show that is about showing off how much the people who are making it know. I've always wanted to do the opposite and make films that dramatise my process of discovery. If I'm doing my job properly, I'm asking the same questions the audience are, as they think them. I don't want to be talking down or up to them, but looking them straight in the eye. It's also difficult when you're making a kind of documentary where it's presenter-led. 'Ross Kemp On . . .' It can sound as if you're giving yourself equal billing to the subject, but I think in many ways I'm making films for the people I grew up with. They might not know they're interested in the relationship between the caste system and globalisation in modern Mumbai, but if we can bring them to it through a film about the brothels in slums, presented by that Grant Mitchell bloke, then I am absolutely fine with that. I'm sure that what allowed those first films to get made was that I was Grant Mitchell the 'famous hard man' going to hard places and meeting people doing hard things, but I hope there's a little more to it these days.

Even now, if the fact that I still have a connection with an audience through Grant means that the team and I can tell stories that we wouldn't be able to otherwise, I'm not losing any sleep over it. I've never had any time for snobbery where the arts are concerned. Would you rather be doing your Petruchio to four people above the Pig and Whistle, or be on *EastEnders*? I know which one I preferred. I approached *EastEnders* as an opportunity to do the absolute best work I could do.

I remember once telling a very well-respected classical actor that I was up for *EastEnders* and he said, 'Well you have to decide if that sort of thing will make you actually happy, or whether you want to make art.' And I can remember thinking, 'I'm pretty sure being able to buy a flat will make me happy.'

And *EastEnders* unlocked so many other things for me too. I'm truly proud of the documentaries the team and I have put out into the world. I hope that a lot of what we made is still watchable today. Sometimes it's sad how little has changed.

I've never given up a source. I've been able to get access to people no one else has because of that. That's my Essex upbringing.

I went to college in Southend, got my Equity card in Southend. I've always joked that when I die, I'll probably get my ashes scattered in Southend.

Farming

'When I die, I want to be fed to them. And then they can grow an English oak tree out of the dung.' It's quite hard to know how to arrange your face when someone says something like that to you.

It's 2020 and we're making a film about people who keep dangerous wild animals in their back gardens. We've already met tigers.* And that's how I met Andy Johnson. He'd been a dairy farmer originally but had decided to make a change. It had started with quails. Andy Johnson had bought a massive barn, about a third the size of a football pitch. And he needed to incubate all the eggs, so he had these heating lights installed. It went very well. He'd become one of the main suppliers of quail for the middle eastern falconry market (as you do). The only problem is, quite a lot of the quails would die. And he felt there must be a better, more ecologically sound way of disposing of quail carcasses that wasn't such a waste.

Now, I don't know how many other methods he tried first, or whether he went straight to crocodiles and alligators. But that's what he uses now. He bought them on the internet and flooded one of his barns. He was raising fifteen saltwater crocodiles when I met him. He also had the biggest snake I

---

* Genuinely, I can't even see the word written down without hearing his voice.

have ever seen in my entire life. Called Princess. I lifted her back half up at one point and I couldn't get my arm around her. Between the two of us we couldn't lift her. One of his crocodiles had a chunk of its lip bitten off, which meant it was fixed in a permanent grin.

Now these are not small creatures. All he has to stop them biting him when he goes into their pens is a bit of plywood with a handle on it like a shield.

'That one's called cuddles,' he says, stroking it. 'When me mum died, she knew. I put my head down on her and you could tell she just knew.' He genuinely believes that crocodiles are telepathic. 'Crocodile brains are poisonous,' he says, presumably in case I'm feeling peckish.

He takes me into a room where he has fifteen baby saltwater crocodiles that will grow to about twenty feet. This room is literally crawling with crocodiles.

One of his ideas is a swimming pool with saltwater crocodiles on one side and humans on the other with a layer of glass in between. When I pointed out that saltwater crocodiles can jump ten feet in the air, he says, 'We'll put a net up.' He tells me that he's swum with his crocodiles. Something I would never do sober. It feels like, as bucket list items go, swimming with crocodiles is never going to rival dolphins. Another idea he had was to make whisky with the water they swim in.

I'm against zoos most of the time. We don't need to keep the animals in cages. Human beings destroy habitats. I've seen what happens in the Amazon when you build a road. That's the end of that bit of the rainforest. The cages (or fences) we need are to stop us from getting to the animals and their habitat. But saying that, as I look at Andrew, frolicking with his crocodiles, I can see there is genuine love on his part. As he's scratching Cuddles's back leg like it's a dog.

'Don't worry, Ross,' shouts Andrew, over his shoulder. 'They're very loving creatures!'*

---

* Yeah, I thought.

Don't Worry, We're Actors

'Don't worry, we're actors.' Hilary Wood, the blue-eyed scourge of uncommitted drama students, walked right through the tube gate at Gloucester Road tube station. This was before the days of tube barriers. And to our astonishment the ticket hall guy just nodded her through. He clearly knew her. There must have been ten of us, who all kind of filed sheepishly in her wake. Her magic spell extended to us, and we were waved through.

The last months of drama school. And as our last piece, we were doing a play set in America. I was cast as this all-American kid. I decided I was going to play him like Steve McQueen's Cooler King in *The Great Escape*.* So I had this baseball mitt and a baseball that I would throw from hand to hand. This was the play that the agents were coming to see. And I had my eye on the prize. From where I stood, there was no point jumping through all the hoops only to be shy and retiring at this point. And it was in lots of ways a zero-sum game. There were, realistically, only a finite amount of people that agents were going to take on from any one visit to one drama school. And I wanted to make sure I was the one they remembered. And in your last two terms, one of the treats you got was to go to Hilary's house. So one Saturday afternoon, off we set.

---

* I wish. There will only ever be one Steve McQueen.

Not many of us had money for tickets. That was the reason we were all going to her house for dinner, so she could 'feed us up'.

That afternoon, I remember these non-sequiturs as she explained the evening ahead to us: 'My husband will be going out. His mother is in. But don't worry, she's ninety years old and an acrobat.'

She'd decided that she would cook a big chilli con carne and we'd rehearse lines in her lounge. Lots of us had other places to be. But you didn't say no to Hilary.

On the tube, we were nervously discussing what would happen if a ticket inspector got on, or when we arrived at the other end. We just weren't sure that her saying 'Don't worry we're actors' was going to cut it with a different guard. But when we got off at the other end, she did exactly the same thing, storming through.

'Don't worry, we're actors.'

It was like a Jedi mind trick.

Finally we get to this house and we're sitting there, and we hear a deep voice calling out and then the door slam and she says, 'That's my husband going out.'

Then we hear a few thuds from upstairs. 'Don't worry, that's my husband's mother. She's an acrobat.'

And it becomes clear that, among other things, she wants to cast her cat for the role of cat in the play we're putting on. She introduces us to her cat 'the gentlest fellow, wouldn't hurt a living thing, I could never have another cat. He's just the gentlest of souls'. And as it walks past it's got a mouse in its mouth, just a tail sticking out. And without missing a beat, she says, 'Could one of you boys deal with that?' So I end up with this headless mouse, and I'm not sure what to do with it. And we're in a row of very nice Victorian terraced houses

142

and I decide the thing to do is to throw it over the fence into the neighbour's garden, and it lands exactly on the washing line and just hangs there perfectly, like some sort of terrible warning to the other mice.

I go back inside and she says, 'Well, you can sit in the Chekhov rocking chair.' And there's this clearly special old rocking chair in pride of place in the corner of the room. Who knows if it's been used in a play, or she got it from a production. For all I know it might be Chekhov's actual chair. So I sit in it and there's this crack. No one else seems to notice. And I haven't got the money to replace it. So I decide the thing to do is to keep sat in this rocking chair, as still as possible, so that it doesn't make any more noise. We're all there talking about our characters and their back stories, improvising around the lines. And I'm kind of using my stomach muscles to keep the rocking chair absolutely still.

She must have realised once I'd left, as I'd been the only one in it all night. But she never mentioned it.

When we'd finished, she took us into the kitchen to cook us all dinner. At one point, as she went to grab a jar of spices, the shelf collapsed and the entire row of spices went in and she fished them out shouting, 'Don't worry! I hope you like spice!' We were so hungry and grateful for a hot meal that we wolfed it down.

The skills I learned from Hilary, I have used in everything I've ever done, acting and documentaries, for almost forty years. She was the best teacher I've ever had.

One thing that has always bugged me when I watch TV or a film is when things arc too neat. Someone needs some change for a phone box, and they pull out the right amount first time. Or the phone gets answered after two rings. A character fills

143

a glass of water without checking it's cold enough. Who does that? I always tried to find little moments of truth when I was acting. Those little physical things that made the audience or the viewer feel that I existed in the same universe as them. It wouldn't always be there in the writing, but it was finding natural moments that allow you to connect with an audience. It doesn't matter who that character is, you have to find those points of connection between you and them, and then the character and the audience.

I've always been one of those believers that the most important acting you can do is reacting. I love those actors who always get the reverse shot, like Sir Anthony Hopkins. You get the actor opposite acting their heart out, chewing the scenery with their big monologue and the director cuts to Anthony Hopkins, because the way he reacts is going to tell us more about this situation than anything that anyone else can do. And it's something I do while making the documentaries too. Because I need the person I'm interviewing to know I'm there, I'm listening to them and I need the audience to be there listening with me.

I have genuinely used things I learned from Hilary throughout my entire career, and life.

I always buy a ticket on the train though.

Tickets Please

'You know this train has another name, don't you, Ross?' said our fixer. I knew the main one was La Bestia, or The Beast, and over the years I've learned to take notice of nicknames. They're usually there for a reason.

'Go on,' I said. Forlornly hoping for something like 'The Lovely Express'.

'The train of death.'

I'm fifty-one years old and we're making a film about the migration route from Central America, up through Mexico and into the US. Migrants run the risk of encountering the Zetta, a cartel formed by ex-special forces who had been trained to take the cartels down. They would come onto the train and take all the young girls away to be put into brothels.

We ended up travelling all around the US/Mexico border, where huge numbers of people die in the desert, trying to make the crossing.

The Beast is a freight train that starts in southern Mexico, right on the border with Guatemala, and carries freight up through Mexico, past Mexico City, and then joins up with a load of railway lines that take goods into the US. Except it doesn't just carry freight, it carries people clinging to the roof too.* An

---

* The goods inside the trains are welcomed over the border. The human beings less so. The irony was not lost on me.

145

estimated half a million people a year try to catch a ride on the train, hoping to get to the better life they believe is waiting for them in the US, often travelling for twenty days. The route is unofficially controlled by the cartels and preyed upon by various groups of bandits.

I saw at first-hand what they were fleeing from. I'd been to a hospital in Honduras in a neighbourhood so violent that someone sitting next to me with a dagger handle poking out of his eye wasn't considered serious enough to be seen urgently. I sat on a rubber ring to cross the river between Honduras and Guatemala and saw what I thought were birds, before I realised they were snakes poking their heads out of the water. Through the night, I sat on a bus packed so tightly with people and their belongings and chickens that you could hardly move.

As the people in Mexico were queuing and waiting for the right train, there was the serious risk of them being rounded up at gunpoint and having the phone number of their relatives in the US extracted from them, who the gunmen would then extort money from by threatening to kill the relative in Mexico.

This wasn't the first time I'd made a film here. The year before, I'd been out in the Arizona desert, interviewing those on the border. When they're moving cattle out there, it's so hot at points in the day that they put them under these massive aluminium covers to reflect the heat back. When they move these large herds, the dust from their cowpats lifts up and it's like this green fog, known as a shog. And if you drive into that, it makes a mess of your car and your lungs, so you have to stop the air coming into your car. We drove through once and it was like suddenly being in a shitstorm. The sun was blotted out by the green dust.

There are watering holes out in the desert for cattle that get separated from the herd. And these watering holes are used by migrants. And they lay under these reflective bin liners so the planes with heat cameras can't find them. I met the forensic officers whose job it was to try and piece together a life from the skeletons they find out in the desert.

But before they even get to that dangerous crossing into the US, a huge proportion of people have already made the journey north to get to Mexico.

We wanted to travel on the roof of the train so I could interview some of those making the journey. Now bear in mind that this is a massive, very long train. Huge numbers of people are injured trying to get on, or they fall asleep and just fall off and die. We brought a guy who knew about rigging in from Mexico City, so we'd at least have something to hold on to, which is a lot more than everyone else on the train has.

We film on this train and it's the height of a two-storey house. It goes barrelling around these curves next to these gorges. It sounds like a beast when it moves. It groans and roars as it winds its way north. Sporadically, someone will shout out 'rama' in Spanish and everyone will duck down to avoid the low-hanging branches of trees, which, occasionally are laden down with the particularly aggressive and venomous Mexican bees. Some of those on La Bestia were pleased to see us, others threw rocks. Even with a rope to hold on to it was extremely intense. I have no idea how people are doing it with no rope and with one hand while in the other one you're holding a baby. Again, it makes you realise just what it must be like where they're coming from, if the risk of this trip is worth it. They are sitting ducks and they are counting down the days until they reach the last stage of the journey.

I was already a little unsettled on this trip because early on there had been an earthquake in the middle of the night that measured 8.1 on the Richter scale. I was so tired that I slept right through it. I came down the next morning and there were bits of the hotel in the road, and someone was like, 'Oh hello, Ross. There's been an earthquake.' But no one had come and woken me up.

And then, as we're approaching the end of our filming, the train we were following was derailed. Luckily it happened near a lake, so they had access to water. I was doing a piece to camera, explaining what had happened and some of the people from the train started throwing stones at us, as a protest against the conditions. It was a sad story of desperate people willing to risk their lives because the conditions they were leaving behind made the risk worth it. But I had promised I'd be home in time for a family reunion and if I waited for the train to be repaired, I'd miss it. So, as has sometimes happened, I decided it was time to get out.

We were about a day and a half's drive from Mexico City, so I sorted a vehicle and driver, and the guy who did the rigging decided to join us because he wanted to get home to see his partner. So we set off and at first it seemed to be going fine, though I was slightly concerned by some of the driver's decisions. He seemed to be seeing things in the road quite late and there was a bit of swerving, but I didn't think too much of it. I was just pleased we were heading towards home, even if it was still a few days away.

Then I see something in the distance, and I expect him to slow down, but he doesn't. As we get closer I see it's people sitting in the road and I shout for him to stop. And it turns out it's a demonstration by the camposinos (farm labourers) and there's no way we're getting through that evening. So our driver suggests we go off road, and we start bouncing across the desert. And it's at this point I realise he can see very little indeed. He's kind of swerving around this scrubland and these trees. We're out in the middle of the countryside, we could have bumped into anyone – the cartels, bandits, anyone. And then, like a scene out of a surreal TV show, we find ourselves in the middle of a windfarm. Huge white propellors turning lazily all around us. And that's when he hits a pothole, and the exhaust falls off. So there's me, the rigger and an extremely partially sighted driver, winding barbed wire we'd cut from a fence to put the exhaust back on.

We must have nearly fatally crashed about five times after that, but the exhaust stayed on and we made it there in one piece. I would end up, at the family reunion, looking around me, thinking about what any of us in this room would do if our family had to take La Bestia. If we got a phone call saying we had to pay money to keep our family alive.

That morning, before I flew back, I woke up early in Mexico City and went to get a coffee, the strongest coffee I have ever had, and spent the entire flight home wired, feeling like I still had to duck branches laden with bees. My hands were shaking so much from caffeine, I dropped a bottle of duty-free tequila and just watched as the liquid spread across the floor.

Punch Drunk

'Enjoy that did you?' A very annoyed-looking man with a mop is glaring at me in the now-empty school hall. 'Half the front row have weed themselves – you can clear it up.' He handed me the mop and bucket. Then he walked off.

As reviews go, I've had worse.

I was twenty years old, fresh out of drama school and stuck in the classic Equity card Catch-22. Because you needed to have worked for thirty-eight weeks to get your Equity union card, without which, you wouldn't be able to work. But you couldn't work until you had an Equity card. The only way around it was to work in repertory theatre or theatre in education. My mum and I had written to every rep theatre and at that point in the mid-eighties there were a lot of them. And thanks to a lovely guy called Chris Dunham, the artistic director, there was the opportunity to get involved with Theatre in Education out of the Palace Theatre at Westcliff-on-Sea, which would make a lovely dent in my thirty-eight weeks of work. So we were off to tour the county of Essex in a minivan, putting on plays in a load of different schools.

There was a play for the older kids about the Osborne brothers from Leigh-on-Sea, who were cockle pickers who rescued

Camping holiday to Spain, 1970.
Already loving travel at age five.

Leaving drama school.
Ooh, what a drama.

John, Jean, Ross and Darren in the time of *The Banana Splits*.

Playing rugby for Brentwood first team while in *EastEnders*.

Early days for the Mitchells – life was about to change for all of us on and off screen.

My dear friend Barbara, I will always love you.

Above: Working for Eddie Jordan's Formula 1 pit crew.

Left: As close as it gets to actually dodging a bullet, Manila.

Below left: Diving in the Red Sea for *Shipwreck Treasure Hunter.*

Below: Honoured to take over Dame Barbara Windsor's work supporting the Royal British Legion on London Poppy Day.

Left: In Kajaki with Snowy and B Company fire-support group, 1 Royal Anglian.

Below: Madness in Madagascar.

Far below: Op Herrick 6, 7 Platoon, B Company, 1 Royal Anglian.

Right: Marta and the boy that could count, Syria.

Below left: Never walk in to the lion's den offering meat. Oops.

Below right: Paul Busby putting me through my paces before I travel.

Above: Driving to the front line in Syria. No idea why we're smiling.

Left: My good friend and director, Johnny McDevitt.

Below left: My mate Dave cracking up after being chased by ostriches.

Below: Proud to be a patron of Help for Heroes.

Very surprised to actually win a BAFTA.

My very good friend, Dr Jarrod Gilbert. I can pick up a conversation with him anytime, anyplace, anywhere.

Interviewing migrants crossing the Libyan desert.

Above left: Me and Renée on a rare night out.

Top: Me and my two girls.

Above: Me and my two boys.

Left: Putting my feet up with Bruno the smiler.

a load of soldiers from Dunkirk, which involved singing lots of sea-shanty style songs.*

For the younger kids, we were doing a play based on Punch and Judy. It started as a traditional puppet show with me in a puppet booth. And then, at a certain point, I steal the wizard's sausages and, to teach me a lesson, he casts a spell to make me the size of a man. I sink down, the booth spins around and then, like I was the puppet made magically big, suddenly appear out the side of the booth with a flip and roll.

I'm Punch. And it's very hard to argue that's not the lead, so I'm happy. And I'm wearing this red-and-white stripy costume with a big hump on my back (channelling my inner Richard III) with long eyelashes and bright red spots on my cheeks and blue eyeshadow. I've even reshaped my nose, so it looks more like a puppet's nose, and I've got yellow socks and black jazz shoes. I look objectively terrifying.

But what you have to know, at this point I think I'm Al Pacino. I'm taking this very seriously. Full method. Who is Mr Punch? Why is he hitting people? It's very hard to read what Mr Punch does and see him as a nice chap, so I'm embracing that darkness. And for some reason I do Mr Punch with a kind of threatening Mancunian accent. Like that high-pitched 'that's the way to do it' voice, but with a tinge of Manchester gangland hitman in there too. So the set spins around and I come tumbling out and I have become Mr Punch and give it 'HELLO BOYS AND GIRLS!' And that's the moment the entire front row wets themselves. Kids are crying. Teachers are shaking their heads. Some have got their heads in their hands.

---

* I can still sing them, so if you ever bump into me and I'm in the right mood I'll give you a rendition of 'It was a sad dark day in June, when the little boat went down . . .'

I try and dial it down a bit, but every performer knows when they've lost their audience and by this point every time I say or do anything, there are all these little pairs of scared eyes staring at me. And they sit there, terrified, until the policeman comes and puts me back in my box.* You can feel the tension leave them as the terrifying Punch man is safely back in his box and the wizard makes me a puppet again.

I don't think the rest of the cast spoke to me off stage for the rest of the week, though I eventually got the hang of it.

Towards the end, we were in the pub one night and one of the old hands patted my hand and said, 'Theatre in education isn't for everyone, dear boy.'

---

* Quite where I belong.

Probably the Best Man
I Ever Met

As he entered the room, the women broke into spontaneous applause. They cheered and whooped. He was embarrassed, raised his hands, smiling for them to stop. But you could see from the way they looked at him that he was special. When people ask me who the best person I have ever met is, I think it's Dr Denis Mukwege.

This next bit is going to be very heavy, so if you're not in a place to hear about the aftermath of sexual violence, you'll want to skip a few pages. But I can't tell the story of Dr Mukwege without you knowing the context he works within.

I met Dr Mukwege at the Panzi Hospital in Bukavu, in the Democratic Republic of the Congo.* We were in the DRC to make a film about the violence between the Hutus and the Tutsis which had spilled over into Eastern DRC from Rwanda. Most of us are sadly aware of the genocide that occurred in Rwanda in 1994 when an estimated more than half a million Tutsis and moderate Hutus were killed by armed Hutu militias. But what is less well known is that this tribal violence spilled over into DRC, where it continued out of the spotlight

---

* It's a useful rule of thumb that any country that puts democratic in its name almost never is.

of international attention. In the DRC I heard about some of the most horrific cruelty I have ever encountered. I was told multiple stories of the use of rape and mutilation as part of tribal violence.[*]

Dr Mukwege and his team treated the injuries of thousands of women who have been the victims of the most appalling sexual violence, pioneering surgical techniques and constantly advocating for more stringent punishment for those who carry out this sort of appalling attack. He had survived multiple assassination attempts and constant threats against his life. When he later found out that he had won a Nobel Peace Prize he was in the operating theatre.

One woman told me how, after she had been captured and beaten, she was forced to carry 20kgs of the mineral cassiterite.[†] At the Hutu camp she saw men cut in half with panga blades and heard stories that they'd killed children by swinging them against the wall. After they'd gang-raped the women, they would force the women's fathers to rape their daughters. Then kill them in front of their eyes. If this is hard to read, imagine how hard it was to hear, looking her in the eye.

I needed to be in a room with the men who did this. I wanted to look them in the eye when they told me how, why, you could do such things to another human being.

We go to a prison to see those who carried out these crimes and it is so full that people are sleeping upright. Tutsis and Hutus mixed together. I am taken to a room and told that there is a convicted rapist on the other side of the door. I can

---

[*] The people of DRC experienced some of history's worst cruelty as a colony of Belgium. The practice of cutting off hands comes directly from the Belgian rubber plantations.

[†] There is almost certainly cassiterite in your mobile phone.

barely control my anger as I walk through the door. But then I am confronted by a child. He tells me his story. He tells me he was taken from his village when he was seven. He was raped, and encouraged to rape 'the enemy'. He was beaten, threatened with violence constantly. The only way to escape being the victim was to become the perpetrator. I search his face for remorse. He tells me he regrets what he's done every time he thinks of it.

I thought I was going to meet a monster. But it's almost never as simple as good and evil. Instead, I saw someone broken by what he'd experienced. I've always been interested in trying to uncover the layers of someone that stops them being simply good or bad. What are the life events that have formed them? What choices did they have? Because I've met so many people over the years who have done things I could never conceive of. But when your range of choices are narrow enough, how can any of us know how we would act?

It's very easy to judge someone else's choices without fully understanding how narrow their range of options were.

That's one of the things that leaving my own bubble shows me time and time again. I've been all around the world, I've seen all sorts of conflict and I've seen people forced from their homes. I've sat in a brothel in Libya and listened to young migrant girls, girls too young to have to know about things like brothels, as they've told me how they would be dragged into the desert by men who didn't want to have to pay. I'll never forget the smell of camel hoof cooking in the pot and sweat and unchanged sheets. I've sat and watched a woman in tears as she tells me that the two small boys she is with don't know yet that their mother drowned the night before. Or the woman who was forced to give birth in a toilet and whose baby survived only one week.

When I see people making arguments over something like immigration with statistics, I try not to just see statistics. I try to remember every single person I've interviewed telling me how they fled their home. I try to think what I would do to ensure my family's safety, what borders I would not cross, what money I would not pay to someone who told me they could get them to safety. I will never be able to truly understand a fraction of what they've been through. But I know it's all connected. There are kids having drugs sewn inside them so that someone in the West can have their Friday-night fun. Our smartphones are full of minerals with children's fingerprints all over them. The same oil that goes into our cars leaks into the dead mangrove swamps in Nigeria.

There is not a here and a there. A them and us. Or, if there is, it quickly loses any useful separation. We are human beings, and it is our duty to stop suffering when we see it. We just have to be brave enough to look. In the middle of the worst cruelty I could imagine, I found the best man I have ever met.

Probably the Worst Man
I Ever Met

I've been angry before. But this was different. I sat there and I knew without a doubt that the world would be a better place without this man in it.

It was 2013 and we were in India, making a documentary about people traffickers, when we heard that there was a senior man who would be willing to be interviewed by us. Mr Khan.

We were out in the forest, just a couple of huts, where we'd been told to meet him. We'd been waiting for about an hour when this figure stepped out from the treeline. I don't know what I'd been expecting but it wasn't this slender, young-looking man in a baseball cap with rings on his fingers. He started out by convincing girls from the village that he was going to marry them, then he'd take them to the cities – at which point he would sell them on. Seven years later, he said he now had a network of seventy-five people traffickers working under him. Despite more than twenty-five active investigations against him, he had never been charged with anything.

When I asked how many girls he had trafficked, he said three or four thousand. As he described how they would go to poor communities and look for 'real beauties', I could feel my hands making themselves into fists. He described how the girls were auctioned to the highest bidder. The most a girl had ever fetched was £8,500. He denied he had ever sold a girl as young as nine but admitted to having sold many twelve-year-olds.

He described how girls who tried to run away or 'were trouble' would be killed and buried in the country. He bribed the police to look the other way. When I asked him how many girls, he replied between four and five hundred. As he spoke, he looked down at the ground, his baseball cap pulled low over his face. It was just numbers. Merchandise. He could have been telling me about containers of fruit. When I asked him whether he would continue to kill girls, he said, 'If I'm having problems, I'll have to carry on killing.' And he looked sorry for himself and a tear rolled down his cheek. I could just about take everything up until that point, but I couldn't take his self-pity. I told the fixer to get him out of my sight.

It's one of the few times I've ever stopped an interview. My translator, who was a criminologist, was in shock. As she was translating, she was crying at what she was hearing. Afterwards, we both sat in tears.

I always try to see the point of view of those we're making a film about. So often, all around the world, you see the same patterns of poverty and desperation, the lack of options. The same circumstances again and again that lead to crime and gangs. But in that moment, as I thought of the girls he had killed and trafficked, their families who would never know what happened, of the endless ripples of human misery that came out of this man and the things he did, I just felt sick.

A Fly

I am as sick and miserable as I have ever been.

I am forty-three years old, sat on half a metal oilcan in Afghanistan, feeling as if the world has fallen out of my arse. The porridge of human waste and misery below me is stained purple in the light of the red headtorch, which I am wearing so snipers won't be able to see me. I'm slumped on this can, over a pit of unimaginable filth. It's unpleasant at the best of times, but right now, it's arguably the worst thing in the universe. Something catches my eye and it's a fly that is taking off from a visit to the contents of the oilcan beneath me.

I kind of watch it lazily circling up, between my legs, then it comes and lands at the corner of my mouth. I'm too weak to even swing my hand at it. I can remember thinking it would be OK, as long as it didn't try and actually crawl into my mouth. So I just leave it there, poking away at me. That was a low point.

Diarrhoea and vomiting (D&V) took more troops off the battlefields in Afghanistan than anything else. One of the reasons was that people who smoked were licking their fingers and pinching their cigarettes off. Or passing sweets around. That's not a good combination with the kinds of sanitation there was out there. It got to a stage where the swill was so bad that they couldn't set fire to it with petrol. I'm not a doctor, but that's a bad sign.

In the early days, whenever I went to the toilet, soldiers got their camera phones out. I dread to think how many pictures there are of me squatting over a hole in the ground. When we first arrived with the troops, there was quite a lot of piss-taking. Snakes put in the sleeping bag, scorpions and camel spiders in my boots. One bloke had drawn a (quite good) picture of me holding a water pistol that they printed off and left about. But that stopped by the time we filmed the second series, because they realised that we'd been spending a lot of time on the front line. They saw that we were trying to tell some sort of truth about their experiences.

You did not want to be ill in Afghanistan. It was hard enough when you were in peak condition. Afghanistan has the most extreme temperature differential of any country on the planet. The first thing that hit me when I went out there was the heat. Like something solid. It hurts to breathe. It's a heavy sheet draped over you. You sweat just standing there.

The DEET we used to get rid of mosquitos was so strong it melted the strap of my watch. And it didn't get rid of the mosquitos. The sweat combines with the DEET and rolls into your eyes, and gets into every little cut and graze and stings. And there are a lot of things that cut you in Afghanistan. It's as if the land is telling you it doesn't want you there.

You'd be covered in sweat and scratches. Every plant has got barbs or prickles. You'd sit down for a rest and there'd immediately be something sticking into you. Everything is sore from sweat and chafing. Your hands have cracked from using the alcohol hand gel.

Everything in Afghanistan feels like a tougher version of itself. If a fly lands on you and you slap it, it just looks up at you as if to say, 'Is that all you've got?'

Before we'd gone out to Afghanistan, we'd trained on Salisbury Plain. Mainly crawling through freezing cold water, weirdly. But the thinking is, it's about overcoming discomfort, not specific to the temperature.

It was so hot that your ration pack would cook from the heat of your body. You'd have it in a pouch behind the ceramic plate in your body armour. It was boil in the bag, but you were the bag. My favourite ration pack was the Chicken Tikka masala. I'd search it out. You'd remove it from your pouch in your body armour and it would be cooked. And you'd sit and you'd eat it and it would be the best moment of your day. I'd go as far as saying it was up there with the best moment of any day I've ever had. Not all the food was something to look forward to though.*

Often, you'd open your ration pack and there'd be a couple of chocolate bars which were now chocolate soup. All the food was too salty for the temperature conditions. Biscuits brown is, perhaps unsurprisingly, a brown salty biscuit. It comes in a shiny purple packet, and you're supposed to spread something on it, usually a fishy paste made from eyes and tails. Exactly what you want in forty-degree heat. It's dry and stodgy and salty and it blocks your insides up almost as soon as you look at it. There are rumours it was designed to lower

---

* I was able to give testimony on just how bad the ration packs were in the early days compared to all the other armies out there. I went in to talk to a House of Commons committee. They'd been designed for a war in a European context. And I was honest about how unsuitable they were for fighting in forty-degree heat.

libido too. Though I have to say that I'm not sure who is out there under fire and feeling randy.* Napoleon may have said an army marches on its stomach but I'm not sure he'd have issued biscuits brown.

Another time we're out in these Jackal vehicles, which are armoured cars with a gun on the back. We start taking incoming fire from the Taliban and we draw up into this compound to take cover. And I need to go. So I rush in there with a John bag that you're meant to collect your number twos in.† I go into as private a place as I can find, which is like a little dark room off to the side, and I start to fill (and I do mean fill) the bag. As my eyes get accustomed to the dark, I get the sense that someone is watching me, and I look up and there's a goat eyeing me up. Not doing anything. There are RPGs cracking and thumping outside. And then there's another goat, and a sheep and another sheep and a chicken. And none of them are doing anything, they're just watching me. I couldn't help but feel this was the strangest audience I had ever had. There was no applause when I finished my performance, just a sympathetic 'baa'.

The only time I have ever felt anywhere near as rough was years later, when I was caught short in a remote village in Madagascar.

We got to a village where they'd never seen white people before and we had to pay a witch doctor to get around the bad luck of us being there. I was halfway through an interview

---

* Some people might and I don't judge, but I can't think of anything less sexy than lying face down in an irrigation ditch while someone tries to kill you.

† The toilet number system was essentially ill equipped to deal with what was coming out of us over there. Number Three?

with one of the members of the village about the terrible raids on their precious zebus (cattle) they'd been experiencing. My stomach went and I knew I had to go. There were no toilets. And I was searching for the place that people used for the toilet.

I had started and it wasn't one of those times I could stop. All of a sudden, an old lady comes out of the undergrowth and stands watching me. I wasn't quite sure of the etiquette, so I tried to keep a neutral expression. Then an old bloke joins her. Another nod. Then some kids. By the time I'm ready for my wet wipes, there are about twenty people stood around me. When I finally pulled up my shorts, they all broke into spontaneous applause.

There's no mummy to look after you when you're ill out on the ground. No one to put a flannel on your head and fetch you glasses of water. You're on your own.

Rugby Trip

I am sick and I want my mum. I'm in bed and surrounded by flu medicine and tissues. I fall in and out of sleep, when suddenly I am woken up with three blokes in my bedroom. I must have left a window open somewhere and my mate Tony and some of the other lads have climbed in.

'Right, we've got to go. We've got your blazer. Where's your kit? Let's go.'

'Boys, honestly, I'm really sick. I can't go.'

'No,' says Tony. 'You're coming. We need you. Get your passport.' I groan and crawl out of bed.

We were supposed to fly to Belfast and play four games, all across the Easter weekend. I was in the first team, and I was one of the few first team players who was due to go. A big chunk of the team were Campion Old Boys, who had played rugby for the local Catholic school, which at the time was one of the best rugby schools in the country.

As I get dressed, the boys pack my bag and then they're literally lifting me up into the minivan parked outside the house. I fall asleep in the van, curled up on three seats at the back, shivering. Then they wake me up and we're at the airport. 'Ross, will you have a pint of Guinness?' Now what I actually want is a honey and lemon, so I just shake my head and try and go back to sleep. We get on the plane, and everyone's drinking constantly. I'm the only one who isn't.

When we get there, I go straight to the hotel room and fall asleep. They go to the hotel bar and carry on drinking. Our first game is the next morning. The next day, I get up and they show me the stockings and suspenders I have to play my first game in as I'm a tour 'virgin' with this team. So, there I am, feeling dreadful, trying to run down the wing in stockings and suspenders, which don't lend themselves to that. It was a real *Rocky Horror* show. But the thing was, I was the only one on both teams not still drunk from the night before. So I think I scored about three tries. And I'm feeling a little bit better. I make it to the end of the game, and I think I even tried a beer that night, just to see, but I wasn't ready for that quite yet. So again, they all head out on the lash, and I head back to the hotel to sleep.

The next day, we're playing a team where the players are Royal Ulster Constabulary. And me and my mate Shawn had this go-to move, where we'd switch the ball, and it would almost always work. So we try and run this move and, before we even get started, someone has broken away from the tail of the lineout and this RUC sergeant comes and hits me in the head at full tilt. And I'm down in the mud, seeing stars. I try and stand up but I'm like Bambi on the ice. And when I do stand up, they all shout, 'He's up!' and when I fall back down because I'm so out of it they shout, 'He's down!' This happens about three times. And then finally I'm just sitting down in the mud and the guy who'd clocked me comes jogging past and winks and says in his thick Ulster accent, 'Welcome to Port Rush.'

I played rugby from the age of ten into my forties. I'd first encountered it on those caravan holidays to Wales, where local kids were throwing the ball about on the beach. And I was lucky that Essex had a real rugby culture, as a lot of Welsh teachers went to work there. I carried a rugby ball with me wherever I went. I'd go out onto the field at the back of our house and kick the ball into the air again and again, practising catching. Once, I kicked the ball up without looking and came around to our very concerned dog licking my face and a big bump on my head with a massive branch lying next to me.

Rugby was the one constant during periods of huge turmoil and I truly believe it kept me grounded. It didn't matter what else was going on in my life, it was somewhere I could go and be myself, a haven. It was where I learned to lose and win. To fail and keep going.

We put a lot of store by success in life. But how you react to failures is much more important. I've learned more from my failures than from my successes. A year after we won a BAFTA, we were nominated for two and didn't win either of them. I think dealing with that sense of failure was much more instructive than the year we won.

Acting, too, is such a subjective trade. How good you are doesn't automatically translate into the biggest career. Most of the time, especially when you're starting out, you're not going to be the one they're looking for. You'll lose a lot more than you win.

There's a real meritocracy to most sports but to rugby in particular. If you can play, it doesn't matter what you've got in your bank account, it doesn't matter if you're a plumber or a banker, you just do your thing. Also, when you're in television, there's often so much out of your control, so many layers of politics, that stripping things down to trying to get the ball over the line ahead of you and stopping it going over the line behind you is a very welcome simplicity.

Rugby kept me fit and strong enough to do my job, whether it was being an actor or making documentaries. Rugby has given me some of the greatest friendships of my life. And it gave me that sense of being part of a team.

I've always worked collaboratively. When I was an actor, what I loved was that moment when it clicks on stage or on set and it's like you're feeding off each other. There's a rhythm you get into. It looks so natural to those watching, they forget it's acting. But when you work with really good actors, they're making tiny changes, of timing and inflection. It's like you're playing tennis and you're hitting the ball back over the net, but with interesting spin, and the other player has to up their game to return it to you, and you to them. That's when you get a feeling that is unique. But acting can often feel like quite a solo occupation. I remember thinking that when I was sitting waiting to go in for an audition. There's an element to being an actor that is competitive. Because you got that part, I can't get it. One of the things I enjoy most about making the docs is that it's so collaborative.

On the documentaries, I've worked with a lot of the same core people for years. I've always had close relationships with my cameramen, soundmen and directors. The sorts of stories we've told make that even more important. Because we all need to look after each other, not only so that we make good TV, but also so that we all come back.

But that night in Port Rush, probably still concussed, I am making enormous shapes on the dance floor, surrounded by a few of the local ladies, when I realise the man who'd clocked me is standing in front of me. For a moment I wonder if he's here to defend the local ladies' honour, or perhaps he's here to finish the job, and I ready myself.

But he just joins me on the dance floor.

I have made a friend.

How Not to Make Friends
with a Nazi

'You know how you said you're the invisible army?' I say.

'Uh huh?' says Rowdy, the giant Ku Klux Klansman.

'Is that why I can only see three of you?'

I'm fifty-two years old and sitting in a confederate flag-draped barn in Texas while a lightning storm is raging outside. I'm listening to a man called Rowdy tell me about the inherent superiority of the white man. Imagine the most clichéd, creepy, soft Texas accent saying the most clichéd racist things you can think of. That's him. He was a particular fan of cod scientific things, like the size of the white man's brain, which you could tell by measuring skulls. I've never met a Nazi I've liked anywhere in the world but this one was particularly repellent. Rowdy was a very large guy with a visible Klan tattoo on the side of his neck, sandy red hair and a little red goatee. And a massive Confederacy-era Colt handgun that he liked to show off. Him and his mates had little tattoos of nooses in between their index finger and their thumb, which they claim means they've lynched someone.

For an invisible army, they certainly liked to draw a lot of attention to themselves. We were supposed to be meeting Rowdy undercover. It was all very cloak and dagger, we were given a location and then we drove out there and we waited.

Eventually he arrived in a converted bright yellow school bus. Not exactly inconspicuous.

We'd already been to meet black militants who believed they needed weapons to protect themselves against people like Rowdy. It didn't feel like an exaggeration to say that the people I spoke to were preparing for a race war.

I've been to the US on a regular basis for the last thirty years, covering a wide range of issues, and what never ceases to amaze me is the gaps between the haves and have nots. That aside, I still love it there – Americans are the best interviewees you can get. But it's not really a country, it's a continent. There's such huge variety of settings and cultures and experiences and it's all contained in one country. It's amazing that it holds together as a union at all; I'm not surprised that sometimes it isn't a happy one. But it's that diversity I love and that ultimately is its greatest strength.

However, Rowdy isn't a massive fan of diversity. Later, we stand out by a burning swastika, as his mate does a Hitler salute, and he explains that he doesn't see black people as human and gets annoyed at me when I tell him I don't agree. Presumably he's taken one look at my hair (or lack of) and assumed I'm broadly sympathetic to his cause. A similar thing had happened when I'd attended a Black Lives Matter protest and had immediately been labelled as a Nazi.*

We go into his barn and it's got these chains hanging from the wall. And he's got this weird lighting effect thing going on behind him as well, like a rotating, coloured light that makes a kind of orange and red fire effect. He tells me there is a provable collusion between the Jews, the non-white races and

---

* At the same protest I was also labelled 'a pig' (police officer) and a 'pinko liberal journalist'. That, my friends, is called range.

169

the Catholics to try and take over the world. He's telling me about the specifics of the Klan, how his mauve outfit means he's the Grand Wizard, to his right is 'Green Dragon', with his pointy hat and silk sheet that are bottle green. His mate in a very large all black number was a 'Nighthawk'.

He tells me I have no idea about the truth, but that people like him are the only thing standing between the white man and annihilation. There he is with his high, creepy voice. Genuinely 'squeal piggy' stuff. And he's saying, 'We've got the church, we got generals in the army who are members. And nobody knows.'

Nighthawk has his brand-new AK-47 in one hand as he shakes my hand with his other and pulls me in to him. He's six foot five if he's anything,* and broad, and he says, 'You take care now.' He has awful breath and he's looking down into my eyes and shaking my hand, which looks like a child's hand in his massive paw. It was impossible to know what expression was on his face. But I certainly wasn't smiling.

---

* Bear in mind a pointy hat always makes you look taller.

Lover Not a Fighter

I can hardly keep from smiling as I say the line.

Questo è un nuovo vim.

I am speaking Italian, I'm dressed like a sailor from a Hollywood musical. Around me are a film crew and a collection of beautiful Scandinavian women sailors. We are all on a tall-masted ship (similar to the *Cutty Sark*) off the coast of Sardinia. If this is what being an actor is like, I love it. I am twenty-one years old and now with an Equity card and a London agent, I had been booked for an advert for an Italian cleaning product. There's me and another British guy who's playing my mate.

We are there to help sell Vim, a cleaning powder so good it will make any house shipshape (at least, I assume that's the general idea). I don't know how I got in with the Italian commercial people, but I am very grateful.

We lived on the boat for a week while shooting the commercial. We were told that at the end of the week, when we got back to Genoa, we'd have this big party. We were delighted, imagining we'd finally be able to spend time with the very beautiful Scandinavian crew.

By the time we got back to port, we'd been out on the water so long that I fell off the hotel toilet because I hadn't got my land legs back yet. But, finally suited and booted, we jumped over the harbour wall to join the party, only to find that the ship had sailed. In our excitement we somehow hadn't noticed that she'd gone – and a ship that size is pretty hard to miss.

Very soon afterwards, I did another advert in Italy, this time for Bacardi. The director was a lovely American guy called Dickford. Kind of seemed like he should be smoking a big cigar all the time even though he wasn't. This time, it was me and another guy out at a bar, drinking Bacardi, while a collection of beautiful Italian people listened to us, laughing with adoration. I was feeling pretty smug, to be honest. I was being paid lots of money to hang out in Milan with beautiful people. While I had willingly mopped children's urine from a school hall, this felt like far more my scene. A long and lucrative side career of being the English guy in Italian adverts stretched ahead of me.

And I remember commenting to Dickford, it was strange that they seemed to cast all these British guys in Italian adverts, and he said, 'We just can't find any Italian guys who are ugly enough. We need to convince Italians that even ugly people become attractive when they drink Bacardi.'*

I nod along and smile but suddenly I'm feeling a lot less smug about my sex appeal.

I always used to say I'm not a lover, *or* a fighter. I'm more of a tap dancer. But the truth is I've been in fights, and I've been in love, and I know which one leaves the deeper scars.

Like lots of people, I had that intense first love, that infatuation and the heartbreak that goes along with that. And it's like burning your hand on the cooker. I don't think it was a conscious decision, but I pulled back a bit for a few years after that. I had relationships but I held back from ever being so into

_____

* My anecdotal experience is that this formula is true of most people and rum.

172

it that I gave up that control. Partly as a defence mechanism to avoid getting hurt. But also, I think that sometimes, when you give off that air, it comes across as a kind of confidence that can be attractive.

And then I got on telly. Not literally.

Looking back, it's so difficult to think yourself back to that time, the mid- to late-nineties, which was the time when I objectively had the most eyeballs on me. This was back before hundreds of channels and streaming and every film ever at the push of a button, never mind the internet and smartphones and instantaneous access to the sum of human knowledge as you're sat on the sofa half-watching something. This was before DVDs even. So there was basically what was on the TV, or you could go and rent a video. There were four (then five) TV channels, and you watched what was on, when it was on. And a hell of a lot of people watched soap operas. During some of those big *EastEnders* storylines, it genuinely did feel as if the whole country came to a standstill to watch. Day to day, I was insulated from it. I was so busy filming or learning lines. But there was definitely the odd comment. If I was out for the evening, I'd get someone shouting 'Grant, you wanker' from a distance. And then I'd get shown to the nice table at the local pizza restaurant. It was swings and roundabouts.

There was one evening at the Albert Hall when my then girlfriend and I had tickets to go and see The Mavericks in concert. We were in a box next to Eddie Jordan, who I'd got to know a bit by this point and who remains a friend to this day, and he introduced us to the manager of The Mavericks. Everyone was very excited because they'd just found out that their song 'Just Want to Dance the Night Away' had gone gold. I'm congratulating the manager and getting ready to say my goodbyes when Eddie has an idea. 'You know what you should do,' he said. 'You should get Ross to give them their gold disc.' Now this man knows Eddie Jordan but he has absolutely no idea who this bald bloke is. However, Eddie convinces him I'm very well-known in Britain.

This was during the storyline when Tiffany is in a coma after tripping down the stairs, and it's been strongly suggested that Grant pushed her. So I'm the man who pushed his pregnant wife down the stairs. And I'd had enough people call me Grant to know that the public weren't necessarily treating it like a drama. It was real to a lot of people. It was what people talked about on the bus, having a coffee: 'I used to like Grant, but I hate him now.'

So they finish playing their song to rapturous applause and someone says, 'So, we've got a surprise . . .' And I walk out with this disc to give them – the band obviously have no idea who I am – and then, to a man and a woman every single person in the Albert Hall starts booing, 'He pushed Tiffany down the stairs.' Despite the gold disc, the band were clearly not happy.

But I'm not going to pretend that fame was miserable, or that I was some kind of work-obsessed monk. I had a very good time. But I'm definitely not stupid enough to think the sex symbol stuff was anything to do with me. It was the character. I'm under no illusions I'd have had the same experiences if I'd fitted boilers throughout the nineties.

I had fun. It was bordering on French farce sometimes. There was the time a very kind group of hotel staff came to sing me happy birthday with a cake, while a woman wearing only the local police force's hat was hiding behind the curtains. It's one thing being caught in flagrante when you're a teenager, and another when you're in your thirties. I've been slapped, had drinks thrown over me, and once had a car driven at me.

But I've always been absolutely clueless when it comes to innuendo. The number of times I've realised, often a couple of days later, that an invite back to 'fix a leaky tap' or whatever was probably more than that. But by that time, I've already rung the plumber.

There was one time a girlfriend and I had been so overcome by passion in the car while the radio was playing, that when it was time to leave the battery was flat. And she couldn't drive. It's hard to play the role of Casanova when your lover is pushing the car in the dark to try and get it to start, shouting, 'Ross, for God's sake, start the car!'

Azov

'Ross,' says the fixer. 'Car won't start.' Oh dear.

It is 2017 and we are in Mariupol in Ukraine, making a programme about the ongoing conflict between pro-Russian Ukrainians and government forces, and the associated rise of far-right Ukrainian nationalism. We are there to spend time with the Azov battalion, a volunteer paramilitary force who exist to fight pro-Russian forces, which includes Ukrainians and ex-soldiers from across Europe. But they have also been strongly linked to right-wing organisations. So we had hired a car in Kiev and driven twelve hours to Mariupol. After filming with them for a couple of weeks we travel to see regular Ukrainian troops who are dug in on the frontline. Before setting out, we check in with the UN observers that our route will avoid pro-Russian troops. We leave over a bridge that had explosives underneath it. Our fixer is a local journalist, who if I squint reminds me of someone from an Austin Powers film. She's wearing a white puffa jacket. White jeans. Red nails, red lipstick and she was chain-smoking cigarettes with huge lipstick stains on them. We're wearing body armour. She's got a lot of hairspray and a knock-off designer gilet. At various points, a little too late to make the turn, she would scream 'now left!' and then 'now right' with a heavy Ukrainian accent.

In spite of the fact we've checked our route, we are all on edge. The Russian-backed separatist forces have been mortaring the area. And we know that we are driving to somewhere that is more dangerous than where we are. And the Kia we have hired is not the roomiest of cars for four of us and all our gear. We reach the Ukrainian troops and our fixer has a long conversation and then we are directed to a location where there are more troops. It becomes clear they are expecting contact. They have dug the tanks in and there's a fair bit of drinking going on. They clearly thought invasion was imminent. We get out of the vehicle and go out to the frontline to speak to one of the officers, so he can tell us what's happening. Our cameraman gives me the thumbs up and I ask a couple of questions, when there's some mortar fire to our right. Our fixer arrives.

'We go now,' she says. But I shake my head. We've driven all the way here and we haven't got a second of footage. We've all been in some dodgy situations before and we can handle it. I turn back to the officer.

'We go now,' she says, a little more forcefully.

My voice is a bit harder this time. 'We'll go in a little bit. But we need to speak to someone while we're here.'

There's more mortar fire. And then the roof at the other end of the building falls down. And as we're all lying on the floor, she says, 'We go now?'

She stands up and looks down at me. Sniffs. 'Roof is asbestos.'

And I say, 'Yes, we go now.'

The next day, relieved to be back in Mariupol, I have one more piece to camera to do in the burned-out mayoral offices. We stow the stuff in the car. I turn the key. Nothing.

We haven't run out of petrol. The battery isn't flat.

Then the fixer points out that the engine has been disabled via satellite.

I have no idea what we're going to do. There is no way we're going to be able to hire another car, there's no way to get a train, but we need to go home. Tom, the producer, gets the information for the hire car place and our fixer has a long, animated call with them.

'Their system says the car has been stolen and was taken to Russian territory.'

'Well it hasn't been stolen, we're bloody well sitting in it!'

'Can they switch it back on?'

She shakes her head. They don't believe we're who we say we are. And for the first time, Dave, Johnathan and Tom, who I have been in some very dicey situations with, lose their rag with each other. And I'm so shocked at this unique occurrence that I start laughing. Which doesn't help. As the English guys are raising their voices, our fixer gets out of the car and lights a cigarette. She calls someone. I watch as she talks to them. Then she comes back and drops her cigarette, steps on it and knocks on the window.

'My uncle will fix it.'

'Who?'

'My uncle works for a car company.'

I point out that it's the car hire place who are the actual problem and they need to unlock the car. Perhaps if I call them back and explain who we are . . .

'My uncle will fix it.'

About ten minutes later, this old bloke in a cap with a cigarette in his mouth turns up, opens the bonnet and pulls something out and then starts the engine. And speedily we drive away.*

---

* In a not particularly enjoyable irony, while I was working on this part of the book, through a succession of events I still don't really understand, I ended up locking my keys, wallet and phone inside the car in a field when I went to pick up Bruno with my son. About three hours and £400 later, we were back home again, but what I wouldn't have given for the old bloke in his cap.

Taxi for Kemp

'Please don't kill us. We're actors.' I don't remember now if we actually said it, or if we were too scared to even speak. But I definitely remember thinking it. Two of us, sat in the back of a taxi in Belfast, during the Troubles, as the taxi driver muttered into his radio, his eyes flicking back to look at us in the rear-view mirror. He's muttering into his radio in a deep, thick Belfast accent. Now this was only a couple of years after the IRA Brighton hotel bombing attack. This was before the Good Friday Agreement. Belfast was a dangerous place.

I was twenty-one, fresh out of drama school and I'd heard about the opportunity to act in training films. The money was decent, and you got experience of working with cameras. You've probably seen them before. The sort of thing they show when someone starts a new job. They show someone picking up a box wrong or putting too many plugs in a power extension or accidentally accepting a bribe. Well, the ones I'd somehow gotten into were films for the armed forces. The first one I'd done had been for the Merchant Navy about how not to get an STD. They all seemed to follow the same formula. There were three of us – the naive one, the cocky young one who made bad decisions, and then the wise old head who'd been around the block. Now, this did not reflect real life in any way, but I was always cast as the wise one.

Clearly I had the look of someone who had learned through bitter experience. The video was about when you were in port, and to make sure that whatever you got up to, you always used a condom. So we went to the red-light district in Amsterdam. We'd already been chased by the bouncers because the director wanted to get these establishing shots of the girls in the window, but he had a bag with a massive camera lens poking out of it – and that wasn't allowed. The director clearly thought he should be directing the original *Poldark* – he wore a cravat, a brown corduroy hat, smoked cheroots and was constantly mentioning actors he'd worked with and was generally a little bit daaaahling.

We're doing this scene where I have to sleep with a prostitute. And the producers for the film have rustled up a local actress to play the woman. With hindsight, I don't think she was classically trained. So I'm supposed to be about to have sex with her and my line is 'I'm going to put a condom on now', but rather than say her line, in very strongly accented English, she says, 'I'm not lying next to him. He smells.' Now, I was very hurt by this. I no longer lived in the urine-soaked flat. In fact I shower twice a day. I was totally sure I didn't smell but still I go to the little sink in this crappy hotel room in the red-light district of Amsterdam, and I wash under my arms with the hand soap. Then I go back, and we try and shoot a kind of simulated sex scene. And it probably looked quite realistic, because I didn't want to be there, and she certainly didn't.

The last shot was of us sailing into the sunset on the bridge of a ship. Me who used a condom. The naive innocent one, who didn't sleep with anyone as he had a family at home. And the cocky one who didn't use a condom, he's just not there. The moral is clear.

Anyway, my brilliant work as whiffy navy condom man clearly went over well, as I got cast in another film, this time for the army. And this was serious stuff about what not to do if you were stationed in Northern Ireland. Don't rock up with your boots and your combats and your sweatshirt with crossed swords and the crown on it. Don't write your address on a cheque if you buy something. Don't go out and start telling people you're a soldier. It was made clear that this was incredibly serious and that we were in danger.

It was the same set-up – naive, cocky and the wise one. Filming didn't start well. The first scene was us loading our bags with regiment insignia into the back of a Ford Sierra.

We got picked up in this unmarked army vehicle by the actor who was playing the naive guy. But in a case of art imitating life, he'd told them that he could drive when clearly he couldn't. So there we were, driving through Belfast in an unmarked army vehicle with the RUC driving beside us and I was having to go, 'OK, now clutch, now', and I was doing the gears for him.

When it was time to do the first scene, he was so nervous, at one point he managed to pull the boot onto his own head. I think that was the last acting job he ever did.

So we did all these different scenes of what not to do and then it was time to do the scene about not wearing your army uniform out in public. We got changed – and remember this had been deliberately chosen by experts as the worst thing you could wear if you're a British soldier out and about on your own in Belfast.

Now the advice at this point was never to get a black cab, because the story at the time was that you could get kidnapped and shot because the cabs were controlled by the IRA. So we're going to shoot a scene where the soldiers get into a taxi and then disappear. The army had hired a black cab, and they've got an actor to play the IRA taxi driver.

We shoot the scene and then the actor playing the taxi driver is supposed to drive us back to our hotel in the taxi.

But as we're on our way back, it breaks down. Leaving us stranded out at the side of the M2 in the middle of nowhere on the outskirts of Belfast. So we're left looking at each other. We take our sweatshirts off and turn them inside out. But we've got shaved heads, and we're wearing army boots and camouflage trousers.

This was before mobile phones and they must have done something to the radio before they hired it out, so there's no way of letting the army know what's happened. So we decide we're going to have to walk into town and then catch an actual taxi there. We walk for ages, until it's getting dark, and then finally, we see a cab and hail it. And the taxi driver looks us up and down and says, 'All right, lads, where to?' The guy playing the taxi driver gives him the address for the UTV studio where he wants to go and meet a casting director. And I'm trying to convince him not to leave us. But we get to his stop, and he jumps out. And then it's just two nervous actors.

'Shall we tell him we're actors?' he whispers to me.

I consider for a moment how we could prove that. Perhaps I could belt out a Rodgers and Hammerstein number? 'Do you honestly think he's going to believe that?'

I'm trying to remember the way back to the hotel, cursing the name of the actor who's left us.

We are wearing, remember, outfits carefully chosen to be exactly the wrong thing to be wearing when getting a taxi in Belfast. We're huddled together in the back of the taxi and the driver is muttering into the radio, and we can't really understand what he's saying, but it sounds like he's telling someone where he's heading. And we have no idea what the right route is, or if he's driving us out into the middle of nowhere.

Somehow, we ended up back at the hotel.* But we certainly hadn't felt very brave.

---

* That hotel was eventually blown up, but thankfully while no one was in it.

Bravery

'Are you going to shoot me? No one's going to fucking kill me.' It's certainly not in the handbook for how you should react when guerrillas point a gun at you in the jungles of Papua New Guinea. They didn't end up shooting me, so I suppose it worked out all right. But if they had shot me, I wouldn't have looked very bright.

When I meet people, if they've seen the documentaries (and believe me, there are still plenty of people I meet who actually think I'm Grant Mitchell, or the character in *Extras*) they normally mention this moment. To be honest, I was more scared of the blokes with spears than the guys with guns. The main thing was to try and stop it escalating as quickly as possible. I may look like I'm being brave but there's a cameraman filming. Imagine how brave the person looking through a viewfinder the size of a matchbox is.* Unknown to him, he has a Second World War rifle pointed at his back.

The main thing I remember is the heat. It's getting on fifty degrees and the humidity was 99%. All you have to do is walk for a minute and you're drenched in sweat. We're

* Thanks Jonathan Young for always being there and holding the camera steady.

walking through the forest to meet these guerrilla soldiers (known charmingly as Rascals). We meet them and I'm sharing their 'cigarette' and trying some betel nut,* when suddenly one of them lifts his rifle and starts pointing it at us and then the other guy has his gun on us too. And they're saying to get on the floor. Now I've read the risk assessment on the Rascals and where we are, up in the highlands. I know the sorts of awful things that are going on up here. So my first thought is, I'd rather be shot than raped and then shot. I figure I'll just point the shotgun away from me and stall for time. Then they shout at us to get on the floor again. But it feels as if something's shifted, so I walk towards the guy, holding his shotgun away from me, looking him in the eye.

If you'd asked me to explain why, I wouldn't have been able to tell you, but it felt as if this was working, or at least, they hadn't shot anyone yet, so I just kept doing it. Looking him in the eye and telling him he wasn't going to shoot me, half-expecting one of the others to shoot me with an arrow or stick me with a spear. And then the moment passed, and they started smiling.

I've never considered what I do brave. I've certainly met many brave people. And I've definitely worked with colleagues whose bravery I admire. But when I go to a place, I stay a couple of months at the longest and then I get to go home. I get to open a bottle of wine, eat dinner with my wife. I get to kiss my kids. The people in our films don't get to leave.

---

* The cigarette was actually made from some of the fearsomely strong New Guinea Gold cannabis. It's so strong that even the Australians import it. Betel nut is a stimulant, so it was like being pulled very hard in two entirely different directions at the same time.

It's not so much that I go to dangerous places either. It's more that I'm drawn to stories of people in conditions that reveal something interesting about how human beings work, and those places are often dangerous. People who are trying to survive. How they adapt. Crime flourishes when people are low on options striving to live. These are the same conditions where gangs flourish too. Those are the stories I'm interested in.

There was a period in my life, when I was making the films in Afghanistan, when I think I did get addicted to it, to the adrenaline and the extremity. I could be in a pub just over Albert Bridge and twenty-four hours later I was knee-deep in an irrigation ditch witnessing a full-on firefight in Afghanistan. What I saw out there was true bravery.

However I really don't recommend facing down men with guns.

Gas! Gas! Quick, Boys!

I really do not recommend being farted on by the Taliban.*

Rural Afghans in Helmand tend to live in compounds made from the local mud. They dig it up, get it wet and when it dries, it's like concrete. It's cool in the summer and keeps you warm in the winter. It's incredibly strong. I've seen a Hellfire missile hit one and do about as much damage as if it had been hit by a 7 iron.

They're normally a quadrangle, with the living quarters around the edge and then they have animals or a garden in the centre. We spent a lot of time moving through recently abandoned compounds. We'd go compound hopping, and you'd lock off two compounds, get arcs up, so you couldn't be ambushed. And then you'd have soldiers up on the corner of the roofs, so someone couldn't run up and chuck explosives into the centre of the compound. It was a cat and mouse game. You'd get up before the Taliban, sometimes 4 a.m., and head off in a different direction to the one they thought you'd go in. So you'd get your head down as soon as you could. He who sleeps first sleeps longest. If you can get your head down first, you can get to sleep. If you wait for someone else to start snoring it gets harder and harder. So I learned to fall asleep

_____

* We had discussions over whether that should be the first line of the book but decided against it.

anywhere with a pillow of boots caked in mud. I'll never forget the night we found what we thought was a good spot for a kip.

This particular night, we arrived at a compound and it wasn't abandoned. The locals had refused to leave. Their dog was barking, which was upsetting a lot of people, as it meant the Taliban would know which compound we were in. So the atmosphere was tense. On top of this, although they might not be, we had to proceed as if everyone we met in the compound was the Taliban, or working with them.

So we all troop in, set up for the night and then try and find a spot where we can get our heads down. Me and the forward operating officer see this odd structure, which looks like a kind of bed or table made from what looks like the bristles of a broom.* I assume it must be some sort of platform that they dry out poppy, or store things on. But it looks like it will keep the light out.† And that could be crucial for us to get to sleep first. So we crawl under, then wriggle about a bit and start to close our eyes.

But about five minutes later, we hear voices and they're coming closer. Then we hear the unmistakable sound as several bodies lay down on the bristles above us. And that's when we realise that we're lying under their bed. We can hear them talking to each other. I decide that the best thing to do is let them fall asleep. And then we can leave quietly.

But then the first fart cracks off. It echoes around the compound. One of them comments, and I can't understand what they're saying but the tone is one clearly full of admiration.

---

* This makes him sound very formal. When we were back at the base he tended to wear a mankini.

† Afghan starlight is up there alongside African and Australian in terms of beauty, but it's so bright it can keep you awake.

Then a different fart, with a different tone. Then a giggle. Now the Afghan diet is predominantly vegetarian. There's the odd bit of lamb and chicken when they can get it, but it mainly features vegetables, rice, lentils and a lot of spices. It becomes clear that they are very aware that we are under there. I'll never truly know if they were Taliban but all I can tell you is that some of those farts would be outlawed by the Geneva Convention. Eventually we crawled out, gasping, and slept that night in a doorway with my head stuck to someone else's boots.

How Not to Make Friends
in Yorkshire

''Is name is Oolio Inglazzy-ass.' He stepped towards me threat-eningly and I realised that things could be about to go very wrong at this point. This particular guy was short, but he was broad, with strength that's come from working every day, not the gym. Red hair and a Freddy Mercury-style moustache with a nicotine-coloured stripe in the middle from the Embassy blues he smoked with military regularity. He was short but bulky. He'd just been laid off from a super-pit and he was furious about it.

I was twenty-two years old and in Yorkshire, working as a labourer. I hadn't planned on it. But that's what happens when you get sacked from *Emmerdale Farm*.

People are often surprised that three years before I joined *EastEnders* as Grant Mitchell, a rebellious and emotionally damaged bad-boy ex-paratrooper, I served my apprenticeship for six months on *Emmerdale Farm*, playing Graham Lodsworth, a rebellious and emotionally damaged bad-boy ex-soldier.*

Early on, I was slightly struggling with the very specific demands of acting on a soap. I was mainly used to plays, which, unless they're experimental, mostly happen in the

---

*   That, my friend, is called range.

order they're written and in real time. You've also read the play a lot and it's (mostly) the same every night. I'd also shot adverts and training films and had the odd single scene in a TV show by this point. But this was the first time I'd ever had multiple lines over multiple scenes, and I was struggling with keeping track of what was what (when you shoot so rapidly often all the outside shots get done first, then inside shots all together, and so everything's out of sequence). Basically, I was losing track of what the sequence of events was and what had just happened, the continuity. Hilary had drilled into us that the way our characters behaved needed to make sense at every moment.

There was a lovely actor on the show called Arthur Pentelow, who played a character called Henry Wilks who helped run the Woolpack pub. He noticed I was struggling and took me aside. He was one of that generation who had cut their teeth in repertory theatre. The oldest of old school. He would wear a tie to rehearsals. He gave me one of his old binders with his name beautifully written in fountain pen, and he taught me a system where you made these notes, so that you had your lines in the order you were going to shoot them, but also you were able to break down the scene, quickly work out the order they would be broadcast and make sure your performance made sense in that order. I was so touched by his kindness. I started using the system religiously and by the end of my twenty-two episodes I felt like I'd cracked it. Then they told me I wasn't coming back. I had no idea why. I thought it had been going well.

I'd gone full method, as I was determined that this was going to be my big break. My character was supposed to be secretly living in a chicken coop, so I asked make-up to put drops in to irritate my eyes because living in a chicken coop would irritate your eyes. In one scene my character had to blow up a car by a river. And I was supposed to walk off into the distance. They wanted a shot through the car with me in the background. And I wanted more screen time at the end of the episode, so I deliberately slowed down my walk.

When the explosion went off, I was lifted up like a teabag and blown into the river, where I landed face down. Serves me right. The per diems were something like £1000 in cash so I had a shoebox full of money, and they put me up in a hotel until I could find a place to live. It was everything you think being an actor is going to be when you're a kid who has no idea. I had absolutely no idea. People giving you a load of money to run around the woods blowing cars up – it was pretty close to what I'd imagined back when I was nine wearing my ice-cream-box helmet.

It was also a lesson in the logistics of filming. It was a time in TV when there were all sorts of union rules and some of them didn't make sense to me. On an evening shoot up in the Yorkshire Dales we were slipping all over the place in the rain and mud, and I offered to help carry the camera for one of the operators. She kept saying, 'Don't help me, you'll get us both in trouble.' And this seemed ridiculous because we needed to get up the hill, and I was a spare pair of hands. But she was right. I got reported to my union by her union because they didn't want women camera operators. TV crews in those days were male-dominated.

I'd turned up in my dark blue Capri JET 194 W, thinking I was the king of the world and there were certain members of the cast who didn't take kindly to that, even though they were wearing sunglasses and expensive ski jackets. It was like they thought they were in Saint Moritz, not Leeds in November. I'd bought the car the day I heard I'd got the part. I was halfway up the A1 when I stopped at a service station and called my mum and she said, 'Get out of the car, now! I've told them you're an actor and they're not insuring you anymore.' So then I had to wait at the service station while my mum called around to try and find someone willing to insure an actor.

Then, on my way into Leeds, I had no idea how to get to my hotel and I stopped to ask these two girls how to get there.* And they said, 'We'll show you' and jumped in the car. I massively enjoyed my time up north. At one point the *Emmerdale* football team needed more male members. The *Emmerdale* cast didn't have a huge number of young men in it at that point. I have never been a football player, but I played rugby, so that was good enough. At one point, Paul, Norman and a couple of other members of the Housemartins would turn up as ringers and they were very good.

We ended up playing against the *EastEnders* team, up against Nick Berry, Tom Watt and Sid Owen.† We were playing at Goodison Park and I did a Hand of God goal and stupidly admitted to it. I was never particularly good at football, but I could run because of rugby.

---

* Remember there were no satnavs, no apps, in fact, no mobile phone.

† A few years later, I was playing for the *EastEnders* team. This time it was pop stars and soap stars, England vs Ireland. It was pretty surreal. 'Grant Mitchell out from the back to Def Leppard, moves it back inside for Lofty, who plays it through to Ricky Butcher, who scores!' We played at Landsdowne Road. Our goalkeeper, a long-haired bloke, was a bit hesitant and I spent the whole game shouting for him to come off his line. After the game, I apologised for getting carried away, and he was very gracious. We talked for a bit and then, as we'd got on, we exchanged details to stay in touch. Later that night, I looked at the bit of paper and it was Ian Gillan, the lead singer of Deep Purple and briefly Black Sabbath. Growing up, I used to have him on my wall. And I'd spent the entire game bawling him out. Maybe I was just jealous he still had long curly hair.

But then I was unceremoniously sacked from *Emmerdale Farm* and it was the end of my world. But that's the business.

The problem was, I'd been living like every day was Christmas Day and by this time I'd met an extremely nice woman up in Yorkshire and moved in with her, and I didn't want to leave her. But I also wanted to pay my way. So while I waited for people to notice me and beat my door down, I reckoned I'd do a bit of labouring for £10 a day to earn some money.

I ended up working with these builders who were knocking down this old hall. A lot of the other lads were locals, laid off from the pits. They were tough. There were no pneumatic drills. They just had picks and sledgehammers. My job, as 'the southern softie', was to hold a spike while one of them hit it with a massive hammer. I hadn't done this sort of work since I was sixteen back in Essex, when I'd spent the summer months carrying packets of browning up and down stairs for the plasterers. I had quickly realised that I was an absolutely hopeless plasterer, but I was very good at demolition.

One afternoon, I was on a piece of scaffolding and we were removing the pebble-dash off the outside of the brickwork. Now bear in mind that health and safety hadn't made its way out to Essex yet, or at least not amongst the builders I was working with. So I was up on this scaffold tower, drilling the pebble-dash off. And then I needed to move the scaffold tower, which was on wheels. Keep in mind that I'm being paid by the hour, so there was absolutely no incentive to cut corners and try and finish as quickly as possible. But it felt like too much effort to climb down and move it. Instead I decided to keep one arm and leg on the tower and then just reach out one-handed with the drill and push against the pebble-dash to keep myself balanced. You'll have worked out that the idiotic superhero complex that many young men have was particularly strong in me. I certainly didn't feel very super a couple of seconds later as I went flying through the air, still holding a big old Kango drill, which was kind of twisting in mid-air and drilling towards my face. And I didn't feel at all super when I landed on the garage roof two storeys beneath me and broke two ribs.

But here I was, several years later, back smashing things up. My arms would shake by the end of the day. It was hard work, and they were hard men. They all smoked Embassy blues. And they were absolutely militant about their tea breaks. It didn't matter where we were and how far we'd got, every two hours we'd stop for a tea and a smoke break.

One break time, one of them gets talking about what he watched on TV last night and he says, in his broad Yorkshire accent, that he watched that 'Oolio Iglazzy-ass'. And who knows why but I reply in my best cod Spanish accent, doing the lisp and everything, 'Ah yes, Julio Iglesias.' And it goes a bit quiet.

''Is name is Oolio Iglazzy-ass.' But I'm not picking up on it.

'Yeah, yeah. The singer. He's made love to a thousand women. Julio Iglesias.'

Anyone else would have got it by this point. But that's when I see him coming towards me with a very specific look in his eye. And I realise and in a very high-pitched voice I quickly said: 'No, you're absolutely right. It's Oolio Iglazzy-ass.'

I worked there for a couple of months, grateful for the work, and every time I came home and had a bath, the water turned brown as the dust came out of my pores and swirled in the bath.

Fresh Mint

I lay in the bath and watched the Afghan dust swirl brown in the water. I was forty years old and over the coming years, I would return to Afghanistan many times. And it would change my life. But after that first trip, all I could think of was what I'd said to camera after being shot at for the first time.

'You can read about it on the television, and you can watch it in books, but it's not until you actually experience it that you realise . . .' As pieces to camera go, it's not a classic. But I believe it gets across something of the truth of what it feels like to be ambushed and shot at.

I have never wanted to be one of those people who pretends that the things they've seen have given them some unique perspective on life. Like you can't truly understand life until you've been shot at or something like that. All I know is that, for me, my life did change after I'd been to Afghanistan.

I had tried to get permission a couple of years before to make a film in Iraq when we were making *Gangs*. We'd been to quite a few hostile environments that involved conflict, and we'd been shot at, but not in a war in the traditional sense.

I'd been trying to make overtures to the Ministry of Defence to get over there as an embed. But I think at that point they couldn't get their head around the idea that a soap actor wanted to go and report on a war.

My dad had done his National Service with the Norfolks, which in 1964, the year I was born, had then been amalgamated with a number of other regiments in the east of England to form the Royal Anglian Regiment. I heard that their 1st Battalion were to be deployed to Afghanistan in 2007 as part of the International Security Assistance Force. When I told my family that I would be joining them, my dad gave me a copy of a speech from *Henry V* and a poem called 'Tommy' by Rudyard Kipling to take out with me, which I kept in my map pocket the whole time I was there.*

I went to meet the commanding officer at Pirbright barracks. And he told me that his decision to allow me to join them out there would be dictated by how well I got on with the Regimental Sergeant Major: 'It depends what the RSM thinks.' That's when I met Robbo, who was the RSM, and Tim who would later become RSM. I didn't realise at the time that they would both become lifelong friends, and I'm still in regular touch with them to this day.

I often work with researchers, but a lot of the time I think it's important to do this stuff one to one. So I went to meet Robbo and he gave me the thumbs up. Then I went to meet the non-elected minister at the Foreign Office. I met them and I discussed what the film was about. I explained that, for me, I didn't want to make a film about politics or religion involved in the conflict. I wanted to see what it was like for these young lads who were deploying out there. Who'd been raised with their pop tarts and their duvets and their mums bringing them up their cups of tea in the morning, to find themselves up against someone who'd never seen a PlayStation, who had

---

* Though they turned to papier-mâché a few days in, they were my good luck charms.

spent their entire lives herding goats and who had been trained to fire an AK-47 before their seventh birthday. I wanted to understand how they would deal with being in a warzone.

I went straight from celebrating winning a BAFTA to lying face down in a field during an ambush.

We had made the decision to use HD cameras because we wanted to try and get across the reality of war; not like in those grainy news-footage images from the Gulf War. But this meant that we all had to carry a lot of kit about.

Naively, I was wearing the blue body armour of a member of the press and I'm with the radio operator. The blue was probably very useful for them to target while I lay face down in a field. One bullet went over my left shoulder and the next one over my right. And I'm expecting the next one to come and pare me down the middle. And then it just went off, a cacophony of different sorts of weapons all at the same time, while I lay buried face down. All around me the crackle of gunfire. The concussive boom of RPGs and mortars.

I'm saying a version of a prayer that my mum had taught me when I was little: 'Gentle Jesus, meek and mild, look upon this little child. Pity my simplicity, Suffer me to come to Thee. Thain I would to thee be brought: Dearest God, forbid it not; In the kingdom of thy grace, Find a child a little place.'

I managed to say it about fifteen times before we started returning fire. And then, as everyone was firing, another bullet zipped right past me. And this guy called Cookie, who was on my right, said 'Ross, are you alive?' You can hear it in the footage. The cameraman is just buried down in the field, but the sound is running, and it captures the chaos of warfare as we tried to dig our bodies down into the ground.

I said, 'Yeah, I think so.' We laughed in relief and I said, 'Living the dream.' We're crawling now, as low as we can. I can hear the sound of my breath and my heartbeat loud in my ears. There's nothing like that hit of adrenaline.

With time though, you become used to the extremity of it all.

In later tours, we'd often be out on patrol to try and deliberately draw contact with the Taliban.

Because of precautions against IEDs, our progress was painfully slow. We managed to travel a total of 4 kilometres in an hour. I was with five Scots. We were ambushed by the Taliban who were attacking with RPGs and AK-47s. So we moved through the undergrowth towards the compounds. We moved along mud walls at the side of cornfields. There's a huge risk of IEDs and ambush. We broke into compounds, the guys checking rooms, looking for traps. It was a game of cat and mouse, as three companies of men were in compounds, hoping that the enemy would open fire and reveal where they were. The fighting was fierce and close. This wasn't people pushing a button and sending missiles remotely. They were 30 metres away, just over the length of your local swimming pool, firing at each other.

Before an RPG gets to you, you can feel the air it's pushing out of its way. We'd just come out of an irrigation trench and thought we'd got somewhere safe. One of the boys was trying to light one of the local cigarettes he smoked but his lighter was full of mud, so I leaned in with my Bic to light it, when a bullet shot between us, close enough to blow the flame out. We jumped back and looked at each other and then we were all laughing like naughty kids smoking behind the bike sheds.

Often, you'd laugh hysterically, partly out of relief that you were still alive. I didn't smoke but you'd have a smoke in the aftermath of an ambush, your hands shaking from the adrenaline. I remember thinking about what I would have been leaving behind if I had been killed and realised that, beyond a few material things, it wasn't as long a list as I'd like.

We seemed to spend a lot of time wading through literal crap. The people of Afghanistan are astonishing farmers and especially irrigators. They pile human dung and animal poo together in these big pyramids and they fertilise their fields with it. Which means, if you're a British soldier trying to get through a field, there's a good chance you'd find yourself wading through an irrigation ditch full of Afghan poo fringed by wild mint.

I remember very clearly this particular time, there were bullets zipping all around us. And I'm in this irrigation trench. I glance to my left and there's this Afghan bloke with a gun standing very still in the next field, clearly hoping we won't be able to see him.

The Taliban were fighting a war on home soil, and they were good at guerrilla warfare. Afghanistan has been invaded so many times over the last couple of hundred years, they've effectively been permanently at war. It's a nation sharpened by warfare. As I said once in a piece to camera, I'm not sure how well disposed I'd be to thirty squaddies breaking into my house and taking a dump in my garden.

The Taliban knew the ground and they knew how to control the general population through fear and intimidation. They would get children to swallow blocks of cannabis resin and then make them wander towards checkpoints with a cart full of explosives and remotely detonate them. I remember seeing a plane that looked like a bluebottle laden with eggs dropping high explosives onto compounds outside Kajaki and knowing that everything below it would be obliterated.

As a member of the Taliban once put it, describing the difference between their soldiers and those they were fighting:

'You may have the wrist watches, but we have the time.' The Taliban controlled the flow of drugs out of Afghanistan, it's what paid for their war. I'm absolutely sure that a lot of the men fighting were on something. Once I slept on the bedroll of a Taliban fighter not very long after he'd left it. It was a surreal feeling to be sleeping where someone who was 'the enemy' had just been. Someone who might end up shooting at us. Someone the lads I was with might end up shot by. But here was his bedroll. He'd left in a hurry and there was this big shoe polish tin by the bed and in it was a glass syringe and a small block of heroin. There are transcripts of reports from the translators for the US Army who would be listening to the Taliban radio chatter. One night the US troops sent up a silver reconnaissance blimp with a camera on it. And you can hear all these stoned Taliban fighters going, 'The silvery fish. Do you see it? Do you see the silvery fish?' 'I love the silvery fish.'

Another exchange that sticks in my memory is, 'The British have turned up.'

'How many of them?'

'All of them.'

It's one of the clichés of war that it changes you, but it's true. At one point we ran into a soldier who we'd interviewed back in the UK a few months earlier, and he genuinely looked like he'd aged by about five years. Partly it was a physical thing; he was leaner and weather-beaten, but it was also in his eyes.

When I first went out there, I didn't really understand what war was actually like. I had read books and watched films and documentaries, but nothing can prepare you for the real thing. But human beings can adapt easily and what you may have considered extremely abnormal just a week ago, can become normal very quickly.

When I got back to London, I couldn't get over the colours after months of being surrounded only by beiges and browns. You'd fly back down over the UK and as that Tristar would break the clouds, there would be this unbelievable green-and-yellow patchwork. And then the drive back would feel so surreal. We'd get to Earls Court Road and it was like that moment in the *Wizard of Oz* when the colour kicks in. For some reason, I would get picked up by an Afghan driver every time. I wasn't sure if someone in the production office was doing it deliberately.

Twenty-four hours after being in the middle of a war, you'd be ordering a takeaway and opening a bottle of wine. It would take a good few weeks to decompress and get used to life at home. Your senses actually did sharpen while you were out there. You spent so much time adrenalised that normal things at home seemed to be running at half speed. And I was only there on the frontline for five to six weeks at a time.

I was consistently taken aback by the professionalism of the soldiers I was out there with. How they dealt with what was asked of them. Governments are quick to draw lines under conflict. But it's harder for those who have actually been out there to move forward, as Kipling says in 'Tommy'.

I'd made promises to myself at various points under fire that if I got out of this situation alive, I'd be a better person. I'd spend my life being gentle and kind. And for a few weeks I would be. If someone ran their shopping trolley into my ankles, I'd let it go. But after a few more weeks at home, I'd be back on the hamster wheel.

I brought no great wisdom back from war, other than it is a terrible thing. There are a small number of people who gain power and money from war. But the vast majority of people just suffer horrendously. The hardest thing I have ever had to do was when we got home and spoke to the parents of the soldiers who had died out there. To look into the eyes of a mother as she asks you, 'What happened to my son?' There's nothing harder than that.

All it takes is a fancy minted brand of toothpaste, or someone ordering mint tea after their lunch, and I'm back crawling through those irrigation ditches, up to my waist in brown water.

Formula One

'Would you like to see the dogs' swimming pool?'

I blinked. I'd had a few drinks by this point, but I wasn't *that* drunk.

This was 2001, I was thirty-five years old, and I'd found myself working as pit crew for Eddie Jordan's Formula 1 team (as you do). I'd got talking to him at an event and told him I'd always been fascinated by that world. One thing led to the other and he asked me to join his pit crew for five races. It was an astonishing experience to be just a small part of that team, operating in that kind of environment. I think that draws together lots of aspects of my life: being part of a group, whether it's a cast of actors, a rugby team, or a crew making documentaries. I've always enjoyed being part of a team where people rely on you, and you rely on them. The idea of bonds forged in some sort of extremity. And the precision that those pit crews have to operate with was unbelievable. It's like a mixture of surgery and aviation.

Everything is numbered, from the smallest screw upwards. Most of the time, I'm not a very precise man. Although when my life depends on it, like making sure my kit is ready before I go out in Afghanistan, I really can be.*

I was cleaning the rims of wheels till my fingers were blis-

---

* Or, as my wife puts it, I actively make a decision to be a slob at home.

tering. One of my jobs was to hold up a screen on a long pole to stop the fuel catching fire on the exhaust when they were refuelling. Before they'd brought that in a car had famously caught fire after a fuel splash. It was literally high-octane stuff. I had my heartbeat measured in that moment and had a standing still heart rate of 170 beats per minute.

To be part of that whole Formula 1 circus, to see the crowds that came to watch. Getting up at the crack of dawn and then working till the sun went down.

They start the engines with what's effectively a big pneumatic screwdriver. When it starts, it's so loud you feel it physically in your body. It was all incredibly precise and well-rehearsed. Bear in mind that's several million pounds' worth of car, so you want to be careful.

Once the cars had pitted twice, they couldn't come back in again, so your job was effectively done. You'd be watching the screens trying to work out what was happening. In spite of the excitement, I'd be so tired, I'd find myself falling asleep standing up in my helmet.

After the Barcelona Grand Prix, I was absolutely exhausted, but my girlfriend at the time had been in the VIP area with her friend and her friend's husband and they had met these two members of the Austrian aristocracy. She came back and whispered, 'Ross, we've got to go for dinner. These guys are amazing.' I'm back at the hotel and all I want to do is eat something and go to bed. On the way out from the race, I'd nearly had my feet crushed when one of the trucks carrying a race car had reversed into ours, and as I'd been opening our damaged door it had fallen, just missing my sandalled feet. But we're still going out.

At quarter to seven, a pair of old-fashioned Daimlers with chauffeurs in hats turned up at our hotel to take us to the restaurant. These aristocrat guys looked like something out of the 1940s: immaculately dressed and with this kind of upright, military bearing. One was bald, the other had a neat side parting. When we got to the extremely fancy restaurant, they strode in and people fussed around us in that way that lets you know these are special guests. Some people enter a place as if they own it, but I was pretty sure in this case they actually did. We were at a 2-star Michelin restaurant on the outskirts of Barcelona. And we were with two members of the Austrian aristocracy, both of whom had duelling scars on their cheeks. I couldn't tell if they were lovers, brothers, or father and son, and I couldn't think of a way of asking that didn't seem rude. They were extremely witty and charming.

The meal was multiple courses, one of those endless processions of foams and emulsions and gels. The only course I remember was the spine of a sheep, which to me looked like the white fluffy bit of a cigarette butt. I have to say, I wasn't massively enjoying the food, but I was very much enjoying the wine. And towards the end of the meal, one of them leaned over and said, 'You must come back to the castle.' And I'm a firm believer that when someone invites you back to their castle, you always say yes. There was a part of me that thought maybe castle was a slight mistranslation. But then we were driving through a village and they said, 'This is our village.' And then we came around a corner of the drive and there it was. An actual castle, with a flag with a two-headed eagle.

When we got there, they showed us how part of the swimming pool went outside of the castle. Like a moat. And then they showed us the dogs' house. It was two storeys and had ramps up to the second floor. And there was a ramp for them to get into their swimming pool. I reckon the dogs' collars were worth more than my car. And even I knew enough about art to know that the pieces on the walls were extremely famous originals. It turned out a very well-known Spanish artist had once owned the castle. I have never drunk as much incredible wine in my life.

The father and son/brothers/lovers were completely lovely people. There was a bit of me that thought there must be a catch, an angle. What did they want from us? But there wasn't. They just wanted to share what they had with us.

As I sat contentedly, even slightly dozily, in a Spanish castle, surrounded by some of the world's most famous art, it was one of those moments when I wished I could have shown fifteen-year-old me, a boy from Essex, the surreal places his life would take him.

'Ahem. Would you like to see the wine cellar, Herr Kent?'

Up, Up and Away

'*Monsieur Kent! Monsieur Kent!*' A French woman is shouting at me loudly through a radio that is hooked above me in the canopy of a parachute. '*À gauche!*' she shouts. Then after a few seconds, '*À droite!*' As I watch the houses get smaller and smaller below me, I am slightly regretting not paying more attention in French lessons at school.

It is 2001 and I am in the French Alps learning how to para-glide with ex-SAS soldier and author Chris Ryan.[*] I met Chris when he acted as a consultant (and appeared) in the show *Ultimate Force*. It was the first big thing I did for ITV. It was an adventure show that dramatised the activities of Red Troop, part of the SAS. I played Staff Sergeant Henry 'Henno' Garvie. It was a really fun show to be part of. Some days we were firing 5000 blank rounds. It was those games I'd played growing up, except this time there were actual guns.[†] We were filming one day early on out near a shopping centre somewhere in Hertfordshire and about a thousand people turned up to watch.

Chris had done a lot of parachuting and paragliding, but he wanted to get his licence so that he could take his friends and family up in tandem. He told me he was going one summer

---

[*]   As you do.
[†]   Little did I know that less than four years later, I'd be out in Afghanistan experiencing the real thing.

and asked me if I wanted to come along. The way he described it sounded life-changing, so off we went. We fly out to the French Alps to meet up with the instructors (and their clapped-out minivan) who were going to teach me how to do it at all, and Chris what he needed to get his licence. It's stunningly beautiful, *Sound of Music* stuff. Bright green pastures and high blue skies and those mountains rising each side of you. And gradually I learned the basics. You get slung into this harness attached to a canopy, which you kind of get up into the breeze, and then you run off the edge and sit back into this big rucksack you've got behind you as you wheel lazily around up there. You pull on one side to turn one way, the other to turn the other way. It's incredibly peaceful, just the sound of the air in the canopy and the odd instruction through the radio.

Our instructors were locals, and these mountain people were pretty amazing when it came to doing extreme stuff. They'd ski off the edge of a mountain and parachute. They could base jump.

One day we'd been going up and down a gentle slope on a mountain to practise our paragliding. Unbeknownst to us, the other side was basically a sheer drop. When we were finished, our instructor told us he was going to pick mushrooms and that we should drive down and he'd see us at the bottom. So we nodded and I drove the old Ford transit van down these mountain roads, with these failing brakes. And by the time we got down there, he was already packing his tiny parachute away. He had a parachute the size of a kid's duvet in his knapsack.*

---

* A few years later, this very brave and talented man died in freak accident while climbing in the mountains. It's always important to keep in mind how fragile life can be. It's all very well doing dangerous things that make you feel alive, but there can be a heavy price to pay.

So it's my day to do the highest paraglide I've ever done. It's supposed to be about 3000 feet. Standing on a ledge, Chris goes first. Off he goes and literally disappears into the low cloud. About 20 metres from the edge and the chute lifts up from the oncoming wind. I'm next. First, I'm running into nothingness and then I'm in the cloud and I'm going up, and I come up through the cloud base and I realise I've gone up significantly higher than three thousand feet. Below me, the houses look like doll's houses. I have no idea where I lifted off from. And I realise I must have hit a thermal, so I try and turn out of it but hit another thermal. And I'm still getting higher. Now I can hardly see the houses. And I start looking up at the rig, which like all resort kit has clearly taken a bit of a beating. And I see that quite a lot of the lines aren't attached. And then I look at where the seat is attached to the chute and there's a rip there too. All of a sudden, the magic of paragliding is feeling less magical. And that's when the radio starts going ('*à gauche*', '*à droite*'), but I'm still rising all the time.

Eventually I turn it left, then right, and I come out of the thermals and I start to descend. And I can see the windsock where I'm meant to land. And Chris comes down and it's like a gymnast sticking the landing. And I'm coming in and there's someone screaming something at me in French. And I'm coming in too fast. This is grass that's been under snow for big chunks of the year, so it's very soft and boggy. I land headfirst and plough a long, brown furrow across the entire hillside.

As I stand up spitting grass, I decide that this might not be something I'm going to take up as a permanent hobby. Chris comes jogging over: 'Ross, are you OK?'

Vices

'Ross, are you OK?' I nod, absent-mindedly, watching all the tiny coloured birds flittering around us twittering. That was when I realised I should probably have been going outside for air. For the last six or so hours, I'd been interviewing members of one of South Africa's most notorious street gangs. As I'd sat with them as they smoked 'tick' (crystal meth) in specially made pipes made from heating up and stretching lightbulbs. Sometimes for a break, they would smoke the enormously strong local cannabis called Durban Poison instead. They'd also crush up Mandrax and put the powder in the pipe and smoke that at the same time. It was a chemical rollercoaster.

Now the cameraman was taking regular breaks, to get some fresh air. But I was trying to win their trust, so I stayed the whole time. I was having a fascinating conversation with them. Which now I realise is at least partly because of the huge amount of drug fumes I have passively consumed. I came out blinking into the sunlight of the Cape Flats and realised about six hours had passed and it was dawn. I emerged into the cold sea air and the sky was this bright, bright blue. I stuffed myself with food. Then I went to my hotel room, lay down on the bed and woke up a day and a night later. How the gang managed to get anything done was impressive.

I've seen a lot of drugs. I've driven across gorges hundreds of metres high in the Andes to see them making cocaine in Peru. I've trod coca leaves at the edge of the Amazon rainforest, making cocaine that would be worth millions in the US. I've accidentally sniffed a home-made pipe with residue of a mixture of aluminium cleaner and insect killer called Man Down, while making a film in Belmarsh prison, and had to go for a bit of a sit-down. Later we filmed a guy who smoked it regularly trying to scoop up water from the bottom of his cell because he was so thirsty and high that he thought the floor was a lake. I've seen people off their face on uppers and downers and everything in between: speedballs and Mandrax, cleaning fluid and glue.

I don't judge anyone. It's not my job. Though my drug of choice is a bottle of Pinot Noir.*

I was brought up with the old adage everything in moderation. Now, my definition of moderation might have been different to some people's, but I fundamentally believe in that still.

I don't judge other people for having a different definition of moderation, but I've seen too many lives hollowed out by addiction to think that live and let live is a policy without consequences. I've seen time and time again as I travel around the world that the way we live our lives always has consequences. So many of the people in any prison you go to are directly or indirectly there because of drugs. Even if they didn't take drugs before they went into prison, they very often start taking them inside just to cope.† There are people for whom drink and drugs is a way of escaping from a miserable life. We know from the experiment of prohibition in America that there's nothing

---

* I often have a wry smile on my face when I listen to people expounding on the dangers of illegal drugs, often as they're knocking back several gin and tonics.

† Because heroin leaves your system quicker than cannabis, lots of prisoners started taking heroin to beat the drugs tests, which in turn meant they would become addicted and spend longer in prison.

intrinsically better about alcohol than other drugs. In the right circumstances, exactly the same criminality and violence can build up around it. I've interviewed people who make a very firm argument for why all drugs should be decriminalised, regulated and taxed. I'm not sure I'm quite there with them.

One of the worst things I've encountered is the over-prescription of painkillers in the US, which has led to addicts buying stuff off the street which is cut with fentanyl. I've been in a room less than five metres from someone who was cutting heroin with fentanyl and I started to feel the effects. In some cases you can absorb it through your skin. It's that powerful. fentanyl is a man-made opioid. Back when we were making a film about opioid addiction, I found out how shockingly easy it is to buy, just through online vendors. I found, and could have bought, a kilogram (enough to kill almost half a million people) from a Ukrainian website, not even from the dark web, just by googling 'buy fentanyl'. This is powerful stuff, and it's dangerously easy to overdose on. Even just a few too many micrograms will do it. In the US it's estimated that about 70 per cent of the 100,000 overdose deaths are related to synthetic opioids.* I spoke to drug dealers in the UK who were prepping for it coming here by sending their chemists out to the US to learn how to cut it from the experts there.

I've seen the human consequences of the War on Drugs. I was going to four murders an hour when I was in Ciudad Juarez in Mexico. I was out with the ambulance drivers who attended the shootings. You'd walk into rooms carpeted in shell casings where people have just sprayed the room with gunfire.

---

* Not many people realise this yet, but the Taliban have significantly reduced Afghanistan's poppy production, so the West should be preparing itself for an increase in the price of heroin, and therefore more fentanyl on the streets.

You'd be slipping on blood. I'll never forget that smell. The bullet holes in the walls. To call it a war would be dignifying it with more order than there was. It was chaos.

Because there's so much money to be made in the drugs trade, everyone is extremely keen to send the message not to mess with them. And it becomes this kind of arms race of unimaginable cruelty, as they try and convince everyone that messing with them was worse for you than messing with the other guys. When I was over there El Chapo was still at large.

It was the Juarez Cartel against the Sinaloa Cartel. And they were using street gangs as soldiers to control the drug routes. The guns were being sent south and the drugs were being sent north into the US. Brutality had become utterly normalised. The home screen on a mobile phone belonging to one of the ambulance drivers who we rode along with was two decapitated heads facing each other on a plate.

I went back to one of the barrios in Juarez to talk to some boys who were in a street gang there selling drugs. A few days previously an old man and a bus driver had been shot. They told me that the boss made the money. Every time a car came past, they flinched. As we sat there, more and more men turned up and they started to get more and more nervous. When I asked them what had happened to the bus driver, they told me that it was 'part of day-to-day life'. There were so many murders every day then, that no single murder was really noticeable.

There are a few people getting very rich at the top. But it is a pyramid built on the backs of unimaginable misery of millions of poor people. And the violence that surrounds it is horrific. While there is a demand, there's always going to be a supply. Attacking one while the other still exists doesn't work. Nothing that's happened so far has actually dented the illegal drugs industry.

Chicago

'Now, Mr Kemp, whatever you do,' says the stern agent for the ATF (Bureau of Alcohol, Tobacco, Firearms and Explosives)* as we drive along, the smell of his mint chewing gum filling the car, 'do not come here to film on your own, do not get out of the car. There is a very good chance you will be robbed and you will be hurt.'

I nod seriously, hoping my expression doesn't reveal that we've been out here filming for the previous two weeks. We've stopped at a red light. All of a sudden, a riverweed-green Dodge pulls up alongside us and a guy with a shaggy beard and long greasy hair hangs out the window waving and calls out.

'Hey, Ross.' I try and ignore him and hope the agent doesn't notice. But he looks at the guy waving at me, then looks over his sunglasses at me.

'Do you know that man, Mr Kemp?'

I am forty-six years old and we are in Chicago, making a documentary about how heroin has become the drug of choice again, even in the middle-class, predominantly white Chicago suburban areas.

Chicago had gone through its coke phase, and it had gone through its crack phase, and had now gone full circle back to heroin. A lot of people were becoming addicted, including

---

* Though it's not in the very long list, they also cover illegal drugs.

soccer moms who were being cuffed into prostitution to feed their habit. It started with soccer moms taking cocaine and then heroin just to jazz things up on a Friday night, and suddenly you find you're taking it on a Tuesday morning and the kids aren't at school. And then there was this whole other market for drugs and battles going on between different factions to control it. We wanted to meet those involved in this conflict at every stage.

We met young women who'd grown up in the suburbs who were now sex workers in the west side to fund their addiction. At one point, a female pimp we were talking to pulled a gun on another pimp and accused him of putting a girl on her turf. Another guy, who was introduced to me as Jerome, overdosed in front of us, having taken a mixture of crack and heroin. His eyes were rolling back in his face, he was literally dying in front of us until someone injected him with something called Naloxone, which reverses the effect of opioids. We walked through places that were carpeted with used needles. One diner we went to next to a brick reclamation yard was called Hoadies, but had been grimly renamed 'Whore Dies' because so many sex workers had died of overdoses there. They had a sign saying 'please don't OD' in the toilets and 'do not use this phone to call your pimp or your dealer'.

And now here we are, in the early hours of the morning: four white guys in a massive bright white Ford Escalade heading into a predominantly African American area. On our way to a chop house,* where the heroin is weighed and packaged before sale on the street. We get out and I'm telling my very experienced soundman Dave, cameraman Steve and director

_____
* I went to a different sort of chop house in Columbia, but that was people, not drugs getting chopped up.

Southern that we have to be extremely quiet. Because we don't know who is watching and we don't want to draw attention and spook anyone. This is serious stuff. We arrive at the tenements, I park up and we get our gear out the back. I make sure we close the boot quietly. I'm not quite tiptoeing but I'm close. Everything is silent. Mission accomplished.

I go to lock the car. And all hell breaks loose. The whole car lights up, there's this loud piercing alarm, the headlights start flashing. It turns out that this model of car has a button, next to the lock button, which is effectively a panic alarm. Immediately dogs start barking and lights start going on. I'm trying to push the button but it's not working. And neighbours are shouting and swearing for us to turn the alarm off and go away. Shouting out 'police, police'. It's only about ten seconds before I find the right button. But then there's just the four of us standing there, sheepishly trying to disappear. Then lights flash and it's a police car. Chicago's finest cruise alongside us and wind the window down and ask us what seems to be the problem as they'd had reports of a disturbance. And I go very well-spoken English and I say, 'Erm, we are making a documentary about early morning birdcall in the inner-city areas of the United States.'* And the police officer, who is everything you think a beat cop from Chicago is going to be, just sighs and says, 'We know why you're here. Just get on with it.'

We are there to meet JJ, who has agreed to be interviewed by us on condition of anonymity. We are greeted at the door by a guy wearing a white T-shirt and a bandana around his face. There is a stark-naked woman covered in needle

---

* This is about as good a lie as I used to tell my dad about who kicked the football through the window.

marks and spots, who is introduced to us as Blondie. Next to her there is another naked woman in her fifties with no teeth. Both of them are wearing plastic hairnets They are naked so they can't steal drugs. For helping him weigh and package his drugs, they will be paid in drugs.

The only problem is JJ can't stop saying his name. And for some reason that means I can't either. It's like that scene from *Dad's Army*.

'OK that was great, but can you just say that again without mentioning your name, JJ? Ah shit.'

JJ describes himself as a broker, or middleman. It gradually becomes clear that he's taken something and as he's weighing out the heroin, he's starting to take a more relaxed attitude to portion control. The first ones were all the same size, but after a while one would have hardly any in it and the next one would be enormous. I couldn't help but worry about the potential for an overdose.*

There was a lot of money at stake. I met a guy who was in control of a substantial number of corners, millions of dollars' worth of heroin, but he went to work in a shirt and tie at 8 a.m. every morning. No one around him had a clue he had this whole other life.

I was again left wondering at the insurmountable task of waging a war on drugs production when the demand for it was clear for all to see. So our final interview was with the ATF agent, to get their perspective on what was happening. And that was when the green Dodge pulled up.

'Rosssssssssssss! Yo, Ross. I've just boosted this car. I'm gonna

---

* I would later learn the very dark fact that the odd overdose is actually *good* for business in the drug trade. Spreads the word that you have the pure stuff.

sell it, you wanna go and get high?' I realise it's Jerome, the guy who overdosed, who is clearly feeling much better. I try to ignore him and the light changes and he drives off.

'So you don't know that man, Mr Kemp?'

'Never seen him before in my life.'

'Well, he seems to know you.' I give it a beat.

'He must be a big fan of *EastEnders*.'

The Funeral

'So you just look at that and imagine that's the funeral in the distance.' They'd fixed a square of white card to the tree in front of me. I was back on set in my Grant Mitchell outfit of leather jacket and jeans. I still remember that first morning when the lovely *EastEnders* costume guy, Peter, had taken me to a department store to buy my first leather jacket for the first screen appearance. I remember, because that morning was the first time I'd ever eaten smoked salmon and scrambled eggs.* In our house, salmon came in chunks in a tin. But we went for breakfast at Harvey Nichols (the first time I'd ever been there too) after buying the jacket and, slightly stumped by the options, I asked Peter what he was having, and he said, 'Smoked salmon and scrambled eggs.' Grant and his leather jacket would change my life forever, but probably no more than discovering smoked salmon and scrambled eggs.

The journey to earn my leather jacket had been drawn out.

To begin with, I'm almost certain I got into *EastEnders* only because I mucked up my chance to be in *The Bill* so badly.

I'm screen-testing for the part of a regular PC. In those days, television cameras used to be attached by a cable. I'm supposed to drive off in the Panda car and I decide I'm going to impress

---

* I was twenty-five years old before I tasted smoked salmon. And if you think I say this to my kids all the time, you're correct.

220

everyone by doing an 'Essex boy wheel spin' and screeching away. But I hadn't factored in the fact the camera and cameraman who were in the back of the car were on a line. Luckily the cable came out, rather than pulling the cameraman and the camera out the back of the car, or that would have been sixty grand of camera totalled (plus a cameraman dragged out of the car). But the crew were not very happy with me.

The other reason was that I had to handcuff someone. So, being still very much in my method phase, I decide that I need to be familiar with the cuffs. I'm a copper. In reality I'd have cuffed hundreds of people. I need to be able to look like that. So I'm practising putting the handcuffs on so that they spin around before they lock. And I'm practising and practising, knocking it on my finger, until it's second nature and then, without thinking, I do it on my wrist. Oops. I go off to the props department and ask them if they have a key. And of course, they must have done, but in solidarity with the cameraman I'd nearly injured, they say 'no'. So I had to play the rest of the scenes with my left hand in my pocket. Funnily enough, I didn't get that role, presumably because they felt I was playing the role extremely casually.

I clearly wasn't right for the part of a policeman but there must have been something volatile in me that they thought might work for a character like Grant. Because within months, when Richard Bramall and Mike Ferguson left *The Bill* and went to *EastEnders*, I was being considered for the part of Grant.

The screen test had then been a prolonged affair. They'd started with a hundred Phils and a hundred Grants. By that point they'd got it down to four options for Grant and four for Phil and they wanted to see various pairings. We were bussed in to the set, ran a scene in lots of different combinations, then they lined us up under the bridge, and we had to say our names and our agents. At that point, it started to feel a bit like we were livestock, and almost as if they were going to check our teeth. Then all of sudden someone started singing 'Neighbours, everybody loves good neighbours' and we all sang the theme song together. Even though we knew that only two of us could get this potentially life-changing part, it was a moment of solidarity.

It seems stupid now, as I have to admit that Steve McFadden and I share a passing familial resemblance, but at the time I don't think I picked him out as a future on-screen brother. In fact, I remember doing the majority of my lines with another Phil, mainly with an actor called Richard Ridings who has had a great career, including playing Daddy Pig in *Peppa Pig*.* Now it feels ridiculous, as Steve's performance as Phil means you can't imagine anyone else playing him. I certainly couldn't have wished for a better screen brother. His professionalism and dedication made the Mitchell Brothers what they were.

When I returned for Peggy's funeral, I'd been filming in Mozambique and arrived off a plane and was straight into filming. Grant, of course, has been living in Brazil and then Portugal, so a bit of sun was keeping it method.

'We don't need a huge amount, Ross, just sadness obviously, but you're being strong, you're holding it together, OK?'

I nodded and waited for them to set up. I'd kept in regular touch with Barbara and Scott after I'd left *EastEnders*. I hadn't seen her for a little while by the time I was shooting this scene and didn't know the full extent of her illness. But I knew she was unwell. As I stood there looking at the white card on the tree, I started thinking back to the first time we'd shot a scene

---

* My daughters understandably couldn't really care less I was in *EastEnders* but they're still very impressed I met Daddy Pig.

together, less than a stone's throw from where we were now. How I'd found her retching with nerves into a plant pot before her first scene. I couldn't imagine the pressure she was under when she appeared in that soap. She had the nation looking at her. It meant so much to her. She wanted to get the part right, to pay respect to all the real Peggy Mitchells, to the strong working-class women holding their families together.

Barbara was such an extremely generous woman. Whenever anyone new joined the cast, she'd be the one to go over and make the first move, to welcome them. You didn't mess with her. She was a matriarch. The show was lucky enough to be full of them: June Brown who played Dot Cotton and Wendy Richards who played Pauline Fowler and the lovely Pam St Clement who played Pat Butcher. Barbara was also very protective of the show.

Years earlier, there was a scene where Grant had to hit Peggy. I pleaded with the producers to cut the scene as soon as I read it. We were rehearsing and I remember she wanted to make it a genuinely shocking moment to get across the power of the scene. I was just concentrating on not accidentally decking a national treasure. We worked out a way that I would give her the gentlest of taps and then the script just said something like 'Peggy stumbles backwards'. It came to action, and I 'slapped' her gently as we'd agreed. She went back, like she'd been hit by Mike Tyson, Henry Cooper and Muhammad Ali all at once, near on somersaulting backwards like a stunt professional, going over the sideboard, ornaments and picture frames showering everywhere. It was like something out of a Rocky film. Everyone rushed in to check she was OK and as they helped her to her feet, she just looked at me, winked and said, 'Ooh that was fantastic.' I got bin liners of hate mail for the next six months.

'Action.'

As I stared at the white paper stuck to a tree, I saw Barbara. I kept trying to get back to being Grant and Peggy, not Ross and Barbara. But thinking of all the years I'd known her, I couldn't help it, something deep inside me welled up and I bawled my eyes out.

'Cut. Thanks, Ross.'

As the director walked away, I heard him muttering, 'Was that a bit too much?'

A Slap-up Meal

How much is too much to spend on a meal?

I was a couple of years into *EastEnders* and thankfully too busy to spend much of the money that I was making. So when I got my summer holiday that year, I decided I could afford to splash out for my birthday, take my girlfriend at the time away to France. And we were going to do it properly.

We go to the Côte d'Azur. And we're staying at the Eze Village Sporting Club hotel. This is a very good hotel.

I ask the reception where I should go for my birthday meal, and they book us into the fanciest place in town. We decide we're going to have a meal at Le Chèvre d'Or. It's a big chunk of a former castle in a medieval walled village looking down over the sea.

I'm twenty-six years old and as I'm walking through this stunning village, I'm feeling pretty happy with myself. I think we both are. Two people from Essex living the high life. We've had a salad Niçoise and rosé wine at lunchtime. The weather is perfect. We're feeling like film stars.

But as we get closer and closer to this restaurant and the level of fanciness of the village and the restaurant becomes clear, suddenly my Marks and Spencer silk shirt with a bit of a hole in it and jeans aren't doing it anymore. My girlfriend is looking beautiful in her dress but she's clearly feeling a bit nervous and I tell her, 'Don't worry.'

As we go up the stairs there's literally a member of staff on each stair, in ascending height order, saying, 'Bon soir.' It's like something out of *Monty Python*. As they're getting taller I'm feeling like I'm getting shorter and shorter. We get to the maître d' and in that fantastically French way, he gives us a flicker of a look that lets us know that he knows that we're not wearing Chanel. And we are led to a table in the corner at the back. They hand us the menu, but it hasn't got any prices on it. Obviously, the only thing you can do when you encounter this sort of thing is to pretend that you're totally used to this and, in fact, so rich that no price would be a problem. So I'm trying to use my basic French to work out what's what on the menu. And I look up at my girlfriend and there's a single tear rolling down her cheek. I ask her what the matter is and she gasps, 'A bowl of soup is fifty quid.'

Trying not to draw attention, I whisper, 'How do you know?'

And she whispers, 'How don't you know?'

So we compare menus and it turns out this is the sort of French restaurant where they have one menu for the man, with the prices on. And one without prices for the woman. Except, for some reason, perhaps the hole in my shirt, they've given the one with prices to her.

I love France and French food. I'd grown up eating a lot of home-cooked French-Essex food because every Saturday evening, when my dad was around, my mum loved to cook. We'd have a special meal all together. My mum, my dad, my brother and me. And my mum collected these recipe magazines you'd buy once a week. You collect them all in a folder and eventually you have a whole book of recipes. She'd cook these amazing meals from around the world. Courgettes and prawns with garlic and paprika was not something a lot of people in Essex were eating at that point in my experience.

If it was a prawn, it was in a prawn cocktail and the default main course was steak and chips.* Coq au vin was my favourite food for years because of those mealtimes. She would cook me a Baked Alaska as my birthday cake, and I still think it's the closest thing to real magic that exists.†

So there'd be Sinatra or Johnny Mathis on the cassette recorder in the background and these wondrous smells coming out of the kitchen. And we'd all get dressed up for dinner. Mum would wear a dress. We'd sit down in the dining room, which my dad had created by dividing the lounge into two separate rooms. We'd have a starter and the special glasses out. And my mum and dad would have a bottle of wine (Black Tower). When we were older, my brother and I would have a bit of wine with water in it. So every Saturday night we'd have two courses from somewhere in the world.

I haven't always been able to afford nice food, but when I have, I've spent money on it. I used to go without food, so I could have one good meal.

It was my brother who once discovered the brilliant strategy of ordering the same thing as my dad when we went on holiday. He'd try and fob us off with sausage and chips or something, while he ordered something delicious for himself. So we used to wait for him to order and then Darren would say, 'I'll have what Dad's having.'

It was those Saturday nights that first opened my eyes to a whole world of different sorts of food. We'd have Italian food or Spanish food, but it was French food via Essex that was

---

* Don't get me wrong, they're still very much a Kemp staple. The last time I went to a restaurant that's what I had.
† I need to eat more Baked Alaska. I promised myself when I was a kid that when I grew up, I'd have it most days. I may look like I do, but I don't.

always my favourite. I'll always be grateful to my mum for opening my eyes and my taste buds. And as far as possible, I've tried to do the same thing with my kids. The only downside now is that I've raised a brood of gourmands who don't know that pizza can be non-stone-baked or that sometimes salmon comes in a tin.

I've done the whole emperor's new clothes of very fancy restaurants with tiny slithers of food surrounded by foams and gels and smoke, and it's not for me. I once went to a restaurant where they brought you a glass tube full of tea, not for you to drink but for you to inhale. I never want to be overly reactionary, but I think you should be given something to eat or drink at a restaurant, rather than inhale it. I was lucky enough to spend time in A.A. Gill's company and learned so much about the elements of a good meal from him.

Back at Le Chèvre d'Or, we swapped menus, ordered what we wanted and had a wonderful meal. Even with the prices in front of me, large as they were, I decided it was worth it. A few years later, completely coincidentally, I was taken for a surprise last-minute holiday by a different girlfriend, and we ended up in the same restaurant but this time we were staying there for a week.

'Wonderful,' I said. Feeling like I was going to need to sell a Golden Goat to afford the bill, or steal one.

The same incredible setting. The same succession of staff on the steps. But this time I got the menu with prices. And by this point a bowl of soup was £100.

An Arm and a Leg

'Ross,' whispers Tom, 'do you think this is going to be expensive?'

I am forty-seven years old and we're deep in the Tanzanian bush, driving to buy a human arm and a leg.

I can't help myself, I laugh nervously. In spite of the seriousness of the situation. It's amazing how universal dark humour is in these sorts of situations. You see it in war, you see it in doctors, paramedics and the police and other frontline services. People use humour to distract themselves and to let off pressure.

You know you're off the beaten track when sleepy zebras kind of open one eye to watch you go past, like 'what are you doing up?' We were there making a film in Tanzania and Kenya about witchcraft. It's a massive part of the culture there, as it is in a surprising number of countries around the world. The biggest spell that was ever cast in the UK, was in a field in Hampshire to stop Hitler invading. The biggest spell online was cast by American 'witches' to stop Trump getting re-elected.

It's said that 60 per cent of Tanzanians believe in witchcraft. In 2011, the year we were shooting our film, the Legal and Human Rights Centre estimated that 600 elderly women were killed as suspected witches. It's one thing to know that in the abstract but quite another to see no one blinks an eye when a young man runs as fast as he can to jump and kick an old woman in the head who has been accused of witchcraft. Women were covered in eucalyptus bushes and set fire to.

It functions in very similar ways as it did hundreds of years ago in Europe, as a way of getting women of a certain age out of the way. Old women who lose their husbands are often accused of witchcraft by neighbours and even by their descendants so that they can get hold of their house and land.

But it's especially dangerous to be an albino in certain African countries with a belief in witchcraft. Albino body parts are believed to be especially powerful if used in magic. I interviewed a young albino woman who had survived being dragged out of her own hut and into the undergrowth and having a leg cut off. Her leg bone was worth so much money. Their genitals are said to be prized as treatments to increase sexual potency.

Their ground-up bone is used in the mines, as the local witch doctor would have ground up albino bone in oil and it would get flicked about and wherever most of it landed, that was where they should dig to find whatever they were looking for. Juju is telling them where to dig next. I've heard people say that they can turn themselves into a snake or a bat and come to your house then later transform back into human form. And the thing is, it doesn't matter whether they can or can't, if people believe they can, they may as well be able to. If everyone in a culture believes that something is true, whether it's that they can turn into a snake, or fly, or come back from the dead, does it matter if they *really* can? That is central to faith systems all around the world.

The first time I travelled to Kenya, to Nairobi, fifteen years previously on my way to a photographic safari trip, I'd had no idea that there would have likely been a little bit of albino somewhere in the corner of every shop or stall that I visited. Hair, fingernail, bone fragment. The more you have, the luckier you will be. Almost all fishing nets have albino hair woven into the net on Lake Victoria, so they can catch more fish.

We met a witch doctor seeing his patients who would come to him with their problems. He would throw up a handful of chicken bones, Lego bricks and half matchbox cars into the air and then, based on how they fell, he would diagnose the curse. It was a very lucrative business model. One week he speaks to a man and tells him his neighbour has put a curse on him, but for a price he takes away the curse and puts it on the neighbour. The next week the neighbour comes and says, 'You need to take the curse back off me.'

In this specific instance we'd gone into the bush posing as someone who wanted to buy human body parts for witchcraft. We'd started the day on the other side of Lake Victoria, having crossed the lake on a ferry that looked like it was going to capsize at any moment. We found ourselves at the end of about twenty-four hours of solid driving, bouncing along in this four-wheel drive in the middle of the bush with the fixer to meet these two guys who we've agreed to buy a human arm and a leg from.

So we're driven to this meeting point in the middle of nowhere. As we sit parked there, giraffes are walking past. And then suddenly these guys appear, wearing balaclavas they've made by pulling a hat down over their face and cutting out eyeholes. The only problem is, they've used bobble hats and kept the bobble on the top, which looks a bit absurd.

At exactly that point there's a lightning storm not far away across the bush. It's like Spielberg has set up the special effects.

They're carrying pangas with big notches in the blades, telling us how they cut off body parts to order and put them in a plastic bag before they deliver them to a witch doctor. They quote us 1,000,000 Tanzanian shillings (£400–500). A whole body can sell for £2000. They tell us that 90 per cent of the senior political figures believed in witchcraft. The police confiscate body parts only to sell them on. There's a rumour that the then-president of Tanzania's bodyguard carries an albino skull around in a briefcase on behalf of his boss. The life expectancy of an albino in Tanzania is about half of the national average because of a combination of violence but also the lack of protection against the sun. In the last five years, over a hundred albinos have been killed and mutilated.

I ask them if they feel bad about what they do and they say, 'Yes, but it is what it is.' It's normal. If you have a relative who is an albino, when they die, you need to bury them in cement so people don't dig them up, dismember them and sell them.

It brought home how different my definition of normal was to so many of the people I met. It was very different from stressing out over learning lines in my special folder, that was for sure.

And they've brought the bag with the arm and the leg in it. And of course, not in a million years are we actually going to buy them. But they think we might. We make our apologies and drive away from them and their bobble hats.

On the same trip we went to a leper colony, which was the only place that albinos really felt safe. And those with leprosy and the albinos were having very healthy children together. I teared up watching a woman with no hands and feet balancing a container in a wheelchair and walking on her knees to fill it with water from the pump.

I lost it a bit with the man who was supposed to be running the colony on behalf of an American charity. He had this big Land Cruiser and a satellite dish on the front of his hut and his kids were clearly well fed. And there were albinos and lepers who were starving. When I found that, it was one of the few times I lost it. I banged on his door and told him he needed to feed them. And that I was going to come back in a couple of months to make sure they were still being fed. And if they weren't, I was going to be much less pleasant when he saw me again. I think he could tell that I meant it.

Make-up

'I mean it, Ross, you look like Gorbachev.' The make-up woman is laughing as she surveys the damage to my scalp. You may remember Gorbachev as the man who brought peace to Russia. I'm almost certain he didn't play rugby.

One of the downsides of playing Grant was that certain members of the opposition saw it as a personal challenge to try and leave a mark on the TV hardman. The problem is they may have thought they were putting the boot in on so-called TV hardman Grant Mitchell. But it was my head that ended up with grazes on it that would start off bright red, then move through a dark crystalline brown and then green. And the producers weren't going to be happy if Grant had an unexplained scratch on his head that kept disappearing and reappearing and changing colour randomly in different scenes.

I remember one day we were playing against Basildon away. It was right at the end of the season and if we won, we'd go up to London 1. If we lost, another team would go up. So, at one point, this other team and all their fans came and watched our game to cheer on our opposition. And they started winding up my opposition winger, trying to get him to put one on me. In the first half, I'm on the side of the pitch away from the crowd full of travelling supporters. But in the second half, I'm on the side right by the clubhouse. Eventually, the winger swings for me, and I fall for it and swing back. And we end up grappling on the floor. And a Doc Martens boot comes whistling past my face, close enough that I can feel the breeze. Everyone came running onto the pitch and my mate Micky Brindal dragged me off to safety.* We went on to win.

So there I'd be early on a Monday to give them the time to cover it up. Perhaps it was memories of my mum cutting hair, but I always enjoyed being in the make-up chair. Something about the sorts of conversation you have. And because I often needed some sort of bruise or cut covered up, I ended up spending a lot of time in the make-up chair. I got to know some of the women who worked in make-up really well, and I ended up going out with a couple too.

One day, word had got back to me that one of the make-up women I had been seeing had a recent ex who worked as part of the crew, and he wasn't happy about it. Let's call him . . . Terry. He'd been trying to make trouble for her at work and had said some pretty nasty things. He'd made it very public what he thought of me, and especially her. I'd made it clear that he should steer clear of me and Elstree Studios because if I saw him, I'd have a word with him in person. For a while, I didn't see him, but I heard he'd continued to run his mouth off with horrible things to anyone who would listen.

Now, what you have to understand is, often you didn't have enough time to get out of your costume in between being needed on set. So you'd go down to the canteen in costume and tuck a load of napkins in your neck and hope you didn't spill anything as you wolfed your lunch down. We'd all be dressed as our characters. Pam St Clement still in her very loud Pat Butcher outfits and dangly earrings at one table.

* Thank you, Micky and all my other rugby mates, Dicky, Tony, Jason, Johnny, et al.

June Brown in her Dot Cotton housecoat at another. As I often was, I'm sat there hunched over my baked potato with beans, tuna and grated cheese at a table with Steve McFadden, when Paul Bradley – who played a character called Nigel Bates, Grant Mitchell's childhood friend (who is wearing a mustard suit, a purple shirt and a yellow kipper tie) – comes over and says, 'Ross. Terry is in the bar.' I didn't say anything, and very calmly walked to the bar.

I clock Terry outside at one of the tables with two of his friends, but they don't notice me.

I go to the bar. 'Ross, you don't normally drink when you're working.'

'Pint of Guinness please, Mavis.'

Then I walk outside and tip the pint over Terry's head. 'Get up and see what happens,' I say, very calmly. Because I know, if he stands up, he has to put his hand on the table. And if his hands are on the table, he can't stop what I'm about to do.

There's no noise, just the sound of the Guinness dripping onto the floor. Then there was a faint ripple of applause from people who knew what he'd been doing. Out of the corner of my eye, I see that Steve McFadden is also standing there in his costume, ready to come running in if it all kicks off. Honestly, all it needed was some dun dun dudda duddas and it would have been the end of an episode. Like many things in life, I regret it now, but at the time . . .

He didn't get up. But I was walking back to the canteen when I heard a call on the tannoy for me to go to the second floor, which is where the producers were and was never good news. However, when I got there, I was just told not to be a naughty boy ever again. And I'm sure Mavis thought twice before she served me another pint of Guinness.

Nine Pints of Guinness

I don't know what's worse. Being teargassed on a nine pints of Guinness hangover without wearing a gas mask. Or watching someone with a nine pints of Guinness hangover remove their gas mask to be sick then put it back on.*

I am forty-five years old and I'm in Israel, making a documentary about Gaza and Israel.

It's around the time of Sukkot, a Jewish festival to mark the escape of the Jews from slavery in Egypt, when traditionally tents or huts are built for those observing the festival to eat their meals in for seven days. I was staying at a hotel in Tel Aviv on the ground floor. And there was a house with a back garden that backed onto the hotel. And I'd seen this old lady who lived there in her garden a few times and this morning, as I left to go out on patrol with the Israeli police, I'd waved cheerfully at her as she made a start on building her tent, and she'd waved back.

We'd spent the day with the Israeli police in a very Jewish Orthodox part of Jerusalem where the police had had stones thrown at them and been called all sorts of names, by the people they were trying to protect.

---

* As an aside, there have been a fair few times when I've had my mobile phone confiscated and then a hood put over my head to take me to a secret location. There has never been a time that it didn't smell of someone else's vomit.

The next day we were scheduled to film a riot. Our fixer told us that young Palestinian lads would come down from the mosque on the hill after Friday prayers and throw stones at Israelis from a new settlement that had been built on the other hill. In the middle, there was a very narrow road with fences, where I'd be with the IDF (Israeli Defence Force) who were there to protect the settlers who, as far as the Palestinians were concerned, had stolen their land.

On the way back from Jerusalem, we get told by the IDF commander that the riot isn't happening. We've spent two and a half weeks in alcohol-free Gaza but now me and Tom Watson are on our way back from Jerusalem to Tel Aviv and it's very much a festival atmosphere. It's evening now and we decide that, since we've got a day off tomorrow, we should go out. We find an Irish/English bar around the corner (as you do) that shows old football matches and has Guinness on tap.

It feels like a message from the gods. And as often happens when you've been filming in an incredibly stressful environment (though not as stressful as it is for those who live there), you take your opportunity to unwind. And one pint becomes three pints, becomes five pints and so on. And then we're leaving the bar and heading to another bar. And then we're leaving the other bar and heading to someone's house who lives nearby and we're having more drinks. We get back to the hotel and they're just setting up for breakfast. Another message from the gods. So we decide to have bagels with cream cheese and smoked salmon and Buck's Fizz for breakfast. It's about 8 a.m. by this time and we're just at the stage of thinking maybe it's time for bed. We can sleep all day and get up for dinner.

I get out of my clothes, strip naked and starfish onto the bed. I feel like I've only closed my eyes for a second, but it must be an hour later when the phone starts ringing. I haven't shut the curtains and the light is pouring in. I can't even open my eyes. I just put my arm out and reach for the phone.

'Urghh?' I can barely speak because my mouth is so dry.

'Ross. It's Tom. The riot's back on. Down in five.' And I just shout, 'Noooooooo.'

Normally, I would have my kit all laid out. But last night I was not in that sort of mood. So there I am, in the middle of one of those hangovers when you feel like you just need to keep still and hope the universe doesn't notice you, naked, stumbling around my hotel room, trying to find my gear. It's extremely slapstick, I'm trying to put trousers on before I've got my underwear on. I'm hopping about trying to pull socks on. At some point, I get the sense that someone is looking at me, and it's then I realise that the old lady is still building her tent outside, but she's now looking in at me. And she's not looking me in the eye. I interpret her reaction as a solid, 'I've seen better, I've seen worse.' Then I pull the curtains and finally finish getting ready.

Tom and I meet out front of the hotel, and he looks as bad as I feel. Forty-five minutes later, after a miraculously vomit-free drive, we are with the IDF standing in front of a blast wall at the bottom of the valley. On one side of us, there are a load of young lads slingshotting stones with amazing precision. The IDF are firing teargas canisters up the hill into oncoming wind and the teargas is drifting back towards us.

Because I've got to speak, I'm the only one who doesn't have a gas mask on. My eyes are streaming, my nose is running. It's called tear gas, but the chemical reaction occurs anywhere on the body where there's enough moisture, so your eyes, your nose and mouth mainly, but also your armpits and your crotch too. Anywhere there's moisture. By this point I'm

239

sweating nine pints of Guinness out, which is setting off the tear gas on my skin.* There's also a non-lethal weapon that the IDF use called 'Skunk', which is a kind of liquid they spray at crowds out of a hose attached to an armoured personnel carrier. However, they're firing that uphill into the wind too, so it's coming back onto us. I will never be able to do justice to just how bad it smells but it's a bit like someone has thrown a rotten meat bomb wrapped in hair into a shit factory and the whole thing has gone up in flames. And it's going up in the air and mixing with the tear gas and it's coming back at us down the hill. I watch as Tom reaches forwards, pulls his gas mask up, vomits onto the sand, then puts his gas mask back on and gives me the double thumbs up.

After two hours, things wind down and everyone disperses. We get in the vehicle and the air conditioning dries my sweat. I stop stinging. When we get back to the hotel, everything is closed for the festival but I don't care because I'm absolutely shattered. I just want to go to sleep. I take my kit off, throw it on the floor and get in the shower. Everything aches. I just want to go to sleep. But then the minute the water hits my skin, the teargas gets set off again and I come out of the shower screaming. It's like I'm on fire. And outside my window I'm greeted by the old lady in the garden having a cup of tea. The first time may have been a mistake, but this was becoming a habit. And this time her expression is very much, 'I've seen better.'

---

* I've been teargassed in Poland, East Timor and Kenya. I can tell you that IDF teargas is the premier cru.

Albert Square

Whatever anyone else did, we wanted to do it better. There used to be this idea that acting in a soap was looked down on as somehow inferior. And it's true that the sheer volume of TV we were making on *EastEnders* made it hard to keep track of all the different elements of your performance. Between the need to factor in the various actors' availability, the inside and outside shoots, and the demands of filming three episodes a week, you effectively had to have nine scripts on the go at any one point.

Steve McFadden, who played my on-screen brother, Phil Mitchell, had trained at RADA and had the same attitude towards his character and performance as I did. We both believed that in spite of all the aspects of the filming schedule that could get in the way, we should keep constant track of our characters in the moment. What had just happened before, what was going to happen afterwards, so that we could make sure it all made sense.

If we'd just done an external shot of Phil and Grant running across the square, then before we started the internal shot that followed it, which could often be more than a week later, we'd run on the spot or do press-ups until we were out of breath. There were a few old hands on set who raised their eyebrows at this approach, but we were both of the opinion that we'd put everything we could into the show. That's not to say that other people didn't, but we *really* went for it. We obsessively ran our lines, and we did everything we could to make things run as smoothly as possible.

I actually think that different approach to performance was a real strength of the show. The co-creators Julia Smith and Tony Holland were so clever in that they married up all sorts of different people from all sorts of different backgrounds, so you had classically trained actors of all different generations next to people who had different training, people who hadn't acted before, or those who came out of comedy and had this unforced, natural quality. You had someone like Mike Reid, who played Frank Butcher, who came out of the comedy clubs and cruise liners opposite Pam St Clements, who played Pat Butcher, who'd done a lot of theatre and television work before joining *EastEnders*. You had June Brown who'd come out of the Old Vic Theatre School and played Lady Macbeth and Hedda Gabler, giving Dot this poise and gravity. They were also so good at finding fresh faces to introduce. Martine McCutcheon, who played Tiffany Mitchell, was only nineteen when she joined. She could sing, she could dance. I had a great working relationship with Martine. Those younger actors who were thrust into that show, I couldn't have done it. Martine was great to work with and very kind. She had this kind of thing you can't fake, this natural quality that people just responded to. She also had an almost supernatural talent for learning her lines on the hoof. There was me with my folders and my colour coding, diligently doing my homework. She'd come in, run the lines and after just a couple of run-throughs, she'd know them better than I did. Barbara, Steve and Letitia Dean, who I worked with the most, were all, without exception, all over their lines, always consummate professionals. You had to be in the midst of so much going on. The more the Mitchell

242

family got these brilliant storylines, the more there was to do. It was graft. A lot of graft. Sometimes when people ask me for my entertaining *EastEnders* stories, I struggle to remember because it was a period of such intense work.

You got into a routine, and you stuck to it. You'd have your two weeks off at Christmas and two weeks in the summer. Then, as regular as clockwork, you'd get a cold for the first couple of days on holiday because your body needed to recharge, but you'd get over it, unwind and recharge a bit. Then you'd get back into Gatwick and be there waiting to pick your luggage up, and suddenly you'd be spotted. In the old days, before camera phones, it was relatively rare that someone would be just carrying a camera about with them. Unless they were coming back from holiday. But you'd come back from holiday and they'd have their cameras and want to have a photo with you, with your arm around their shoulders and everything. There'd be all these people who had holidayed around the world, bringing back germs and cuddling you. So then the first few days after every holiday I'd get back to work on the set with another stinking cold. You just had to keep going. I used to keep tissues under the bar of the Queen Vic, which the props guys were rightly disgusted by. But if you were late, or ill, you were holding up the whole production. I could hear Hilary's voice chiding me for being unprofessional.

Early on, I was driving up to the studio.* There had been some very strong winds and there were trees down everywhere. The winds were so strong that as I was driving along on the motorway, I was nearly hit by a smashed-up caravan

---

* I was in Kent, then Essex, and then settled in south London. I'd drive five and sometimes six days a week up to Elstree, which could take three hours. My left ankle would throb from all the gear changes.

that flew off the back of a lorry in front of me. I got a puncture and had to pull over at the side of the road to change the wheel. I was trying to hurry and ended up taking the skin off my knuckles. So I turned up about half an hour late, with my shirt covered in blood, in the middle of a gale, and I still got a strip torn off me.

But there were benefits to the rigid order too. The way it worked was you'd be told which scenes you were in, so if you weren't in one, you could go off and relax a bit. I'd go round the corner and play darts in the bit of the Vic that wasn't being filmed. Or I'd go and learn my lines on the stairs in the back, or have a cup of tea and a chat with Steve. Or go for a gossip with the supporting artists who were regulars, some of whom had been on the show since the beginning. They were intrinsic to the running of the show and the tone. But I'd ask the camera crew to let me know when an episode was being filmed in the Vic, even if I wasn't meant to be in it. The more episodes you're in, the more you got paid. So, if they were filming a scene in the Vic, sometimes I'd pop by in the background and say, 'All right, Big Ron. Pint of lager and a gin and tonic and packet of crisps, was it?' so I'd been in another episode.*

Another way of making extra money was to do personal appearances. I wouldn't pay me to open a packet of crisps, but for some reason I was in high demand. You'd turn up at a club, sign some photographs, and get your bum pinched for a couple of hours. I did two in a night sometimes. I got into a routine for a while, where I'd play rugby on the Saturday and then I'd lie down in the back of the car while my mate Johnny

---

* If anyone from *EastEnders* accounts is reading this, it's a lie to make my book more exciting. Please do not check.

from the rugby club would drive me up to wherever we were doing appearances that Saturday. We used to buy chocolate from the garage and play games to pass the time. How long you could keep a Minstrel on your tongue or what flavour is your Revel. That kind of racy stuff.

One night we pull up at a nightclub somewhere in the northeast. There are two enormous bouncers outside and a big crowd behind the barriers. I get out and walk down and I wave at the crowd. And a loud Geordie voice shouts out, 'Grant! Howay lad.'

I'm up on stage doing an interview with the DJ and the next thing I know I feel a slap on my left shoulder and then one on my right shoulder and I can't quite work out who hit me. But then suddenly these two bouncers are lifting me up like I'm a little kid and running with me back out to the car park and putting me into a car.

'What happened?' I asked them.

'Mate, you just got hit by two pint glasses.' Grant had that effect on some people.

Another time at a nightclub in Chesterfield, they'd let everyone in, far too many people for the venue's capacity. I'd often do a Q&A with the DJ and there'd be this huge crowd. No one was going to be able to dance because there wasn't enough room. But this night, there was a surge, and as one, the entire crowd, including me, went down like dominoes. People were screaming. It was genuinely scary. I got back up and managed to get to the stage. They had to let people out.

Another time, in Port Talbot, we got to this club, which was above a working man's club.

'There's no queue outside, Johnny,' I said.

'Maybe they're all inside?'

When we go up there, the woman who owns it is not in a good place. 'I've got to be honest with you, my husband has run off with the barmaid and taken all the money. We've not really been able to promote as we'd hoped.'

The place is virtually empty. The DJ is wearing a velvet bow tie. Never a good look. I felt sorry for the woman, so I say I'll stick around and see if anyone else turns up. In a cavernous empty nightclub in Port Talbot, the DJ asks me what my favourite food is. And I say fish and chips. It's not exactly Frost vs Nixon.

At the end, three women, all of whom have bigger biceps than me, corner me and won't let me leave. It takes all my strength to break away and make it back to the car. Johnny is creasing up laughing. 'I thought you'd got engaged at one point back there.'

Sex, Drugs and Cuddly Toys

Marta leaned over and whispered: 'You realise that means you're engaged?' This was bad news on many fronts: 1) My supposed new fiancée's brother was the leader of 'The Little Psychopaths of Delgado' gang; 2) She was only fifteen; 3) I was already engaged to someone else.

I am forty-one years old, and we are making an episode of *Gangs* with MS-13, or Mara Salvatrucha, one of the most brutal street gangs in the world, who had originally come out of the civil war in El Salvador and had taken over a large chunk of the US drugs market. We had met Chucho, which means dog, a few times. Chucho liked his guns and he liked to show us his guns. Early on, his sister had given me this cuddly toy, soaked in eye-wateringly strong perfume, but I hadn't thought much of it. You see loads of those toys out there all over the place, in the petrol stations and heavily fortified tobacconists all across El Salvador.* These furry teddies with a little plastic face on a keyring. Now, operating on the principle that you should never refuse a gift, I took it from her and thanked her profusely. And then we were in a petrol station on the way to our next meeting at a prison, and I saw one and I thought,

---

* There were guns absolutely everywhere in El Salvador at that point. Even when you went to go and get petrol, the guy at the pump had a sawn-off pump-action shotgun.

'You know what would be even more polite, Kemp. Why don't you buy her one back?'

We're filming with Chucho and his gang for the day, and when I see Chucho's sister I give her the toy. She seems very pleased. As does Chucho. It's only when their mother also seems delighted that I realise something else might be up.

That's when Marta whispers in my ear. I'm now engaged to the sister. I explain that's going to be a bit awkward with my fiancée at home. Chucho's sister runs off in tears. Chucho is not happy. His mother is giving me daggers, but I apologise profusely.

To make amends for not marrying his sister, I have to lay on a big feast (which I am more than happy to do). Beer and chicken. So we go to the supermarket and return laden with bags. Outside, there's a barbecue, with these big steel drums where they're grilling piles of meat. The whole gang has turned out. There are guns, beer and Mary Jane everywhere. Not always a good mix.

So I'm sitting at a plastic table. And I'm talking to Marta.

And Chucho has got his big shiny pistol out on the table and he's spinning it around like a terrifying game of spin the bottle and looking intently at me. His mother and sister are also clearly not happy.

So then they start bringing out the food and putting it in front of people and it's this delicious-looking grilled chicken with salad. And then my piece arrives. This chicken has barely seen a flame. It could still get up and run away. If I listen carefully, I'm sure I can hear it clucking. It could still lay an egg. I look at Marta's: cooked. The person's on the other side of me: cooked. I put my plastic fork in mine and blood seeps out, making the paper plate red. And I'm absolutely sure I can't eat it. Just the thought of eating it makes me feel sick.

248

And Chucho is watching me, and he waves with his very large shiny pistol, points at me and says: '*Pollo, Pollo.*'

The way I saw it, I had three choices: marry Chucho's sister, which wasn't an option; get shot, which wasn't an option; or take my chances with the chicken.

So I start eating the chicken. Honestly, I can hardly cut it with a plastic knife and fork. I can hardly chew and swallow it, it's so raw. And I'm kind of dribbling this blood out of my mouth.

And Chucho is just watching me, smiling.

About half an hour later, I realise I need to leave. It's hot, there's weed smoke everywhere, my stomach is turning somersaults. As we leave, I can hear Chucho and the gang laughing. We're walking back to the four by four and I'm starting to feel very strange. I'm sweating and gagging and feeling like I'm going to pass out. And we're in this old Suzuki jeep, and I'm sitting there with my head hanging out the window, unable to concentrate on anything but not being sick.

We get back to the hotel and I decide I need some sort of medicine. I'm delirious by this point. I've got food poisoning. I'm going to be violently sick. I'm moaning and sweating.

Marta goes off to look around the shops but the only thing she can find is a bottle of bright pink Pepto Bismol.* So I drink a big glug of that and lie down on my bed.

Moments later, I'm in my hotel bathroom and I've become a bright pink human Catherine wheel at both ends. I don't remember much of the next twelve hours, but when I come to, the bathroom floor is pink, brown and yellow and my face is stuck to it.

---

* For those that don't know, Pepto Bismol is a bright pink American antacid. Not much use with food poisoning but it's all we had.

I was ill for days after that. Chucho's revenge.

That's not the kind of honeymoon anyone wants. Brings a whole new meaning to being lovesick.

Hells Angel

I love motorcycles but I'm not sure how much they love me. A long time into working at *EastEnders*, I decided it would be much more efficient for me to get from south London, where I was living, to the studios at Elstree, in north London, if I bought a motorcycle. So I did my course and then I bought myself a green and silver Triumph T-Bird. One of those classic sit-up and beg motorbikes. Now, looking back, it was pretty difficult to manoeuvre and too powerful to make a good first bike. I should probably have started with something lighter and less powerful (and a lot cheaper). But I didn't know what I was doing.

By the time I'd got into my leathers and my white Arai helmet* and wheeled the bike carefully out and got to Elstree, I was running about fifteen minutes later than if I'd driven in my Golf GTI. That probably tells you a lot about my bike riding.

I absolutely loved it. I loved having a bike and the freedom and anonymity it gave me. I tried to ride it everywhere I could, including popping to the barbers. Now, by this point, there wasn't a huge amount for them to do. But I used to drive up from Clapham and go and see a Cypriot barber who I got on with. He'd shave my head and we'd have a chat and a cup of coffee. It became part of my routine to decompress away from *EastEnders*.

---

* Yes, I had just passed my test.

I'd bought what I was reliably informed was the best kind of lock to look after my precious bike. It's called a disc lock and it fastens to the front wheel disc brake to stop the wheel rotating more than a couple of inches or so. So I park my bike up facing out onto the road, put the lock on and then head across to the barbers. As I do, I notice a couple of blokes who are looking a bit worse for wear. They're pouring vodka into Special Brew cans and smoking. I keep my helmet on till I get into the barbershop. That's another bonus to riding a bike – free disguise when you're out and about. And then I'm chatting with the barber as he shaves my head when there's a knocking on the window: 'Is it you, Grant? Can we come in and say hello?' these two men ask.

The barber calls out that I'm having my hair cut and they should leave me alone. But they're not leaving, so I call out: 'What do you need, lads?'

'Can you sign this?'

So I nip out and they've got the inside of a fag packet opened up and I sign it. And one of them points at my head and goes, 'It's not gonna take him long to do you, is it?' And the barber very politely ushers them away. But then when I head back out to get on my bike, they jump up and come over again: 'Can you sign this please, Grant?'

And now they've got a load of bits of paper and loads of messages to various people. They've clearly spent the last fifteen minutes asking everyone they know what message they'd like from Grant Mitchell. I tell them I'm happy to, but I just want to get on my bike first. Then I'm signing bits of paper and they're still drinking their cocktails and smoking their rollies and they're a little bit loud. And I never mind autographs or photos or any of that because I've always accepted

252

that's part of the job.* It means you're doing something right. Overwhelmingly, most people are very polite and lovely. Just after my first episodes of *EastEnders* aired, I went out with my mum and nan for tea and about thirty people came up for autographs. When we left, I was discussing it with my mum and my dad said, 'I thought that's what you'd always wanted?' And I realised he was absolutely right. If you want to be on television, you can't moan about it.

But back in Clapham I decide that I do need to get on with my day. So I pull in the clutch, kick the bike into gear, rev the engine and give my two new fans a nod. I let the clutch out, and I'm ready to zoom off on my bike like Evel Knievel. Except what actually happens is I go straight over the top. Because I've not been concentrating, I've completely forgotten the disc lock is still on. And it's like someone ramming a stick into the spokes of your purple chopper. And even worse, somehow, as I've gone spinning over the top, I've taken off the petrol cap. So now I have a very heavy bike on top of me with petrol leaking onto me. And these two guys immediately say, 'Ah shit, Grant.' And they're trying to get the bike off me. But in their haste, they've kept their fags in their mouth. So I'm shouting, 'Petrol, petrol. Go away.'

Eventually I get out from under it. I go back into the barber's, stinking of petrol. And I've broken my favourite toy.

He makes me a cup of coffee and just then someone else pops their head around the door and says, 'Grant, can you sign this?'

'Not now,' the barber replies. He can see I'm in mourning, as my bike and my dignity are wrecked. And then he helps me

---

* I've only ever said no once and that was because I was feeding my infant daughters and someone said, 'Oi, sign this.'

call someone to come and pick up the bike. When he arrives, this absolutely enormous bloke who is about four of me wide, he takes one look at the bike, then puts his arm round me and says in a classic cockney geezer voice, 'Don't worry, mate. We've all done it.'

Then he heads back outside, lifts my bike up under one arm and puts it on the back of his truck. Then he picks me up and puts me in the front. I'm not sure if he was a guardian angel or a Hells Angel. Maybe both.

Rebel Rebels

I am not sure what the etiquette is when you're riding up front of a motorcycle convoy with almost a hundred members of the Rebel bike gang and you need to stop. I have no idea why I am at the front but pretty much every one of them is big enough to pick me up and post me through a letterbox. A lot of them have 'This bike belongs to a Rebel. Touch it and find out' on their bikes.

It's 2014 and we're making a film about the biker gangs in Australia. We were there to look at the special laws called VLAD (Vicious Lawless Association Disestablishment), which were there to effectively punish the biker gangs and meant that any biker could be found guilty of a crime just by association. The police believed that a huge amount of the movement of drugs in the country was controlled by the 'bikies'. There are a lot of biker gangs in that part of the world. The Rebels have seventy chapters in Australia, with over a thousand members.

The Rebels are a 1 per cent club.* The bikies believed that just because you're a member of the 1 per cent, it doesn't

---

* There had been this famous riot in Hollister in California in 1947, when a motorcycle rally had turned into a brawl. At some point, the president of the American Motorcycle Association made a statement that 99 per cent of motorcycle clubs were law-abiding. And so the 1 per cent who weren't was born.

follow that you're definitely involved in organised crime. But the police believed differently.

We were going to ride to meet them at their clubhouse in the suburbs, interview a few members about their experiences, then join them in a memorial service at the grave of one of their members, where they'd pour out a bottle of whisky, sprinkle some weed and then we'd listen to a poem in his memory.

I'd been riding bikes for a few years by this point, and though I'm still not the best biker in the world, I have this big Harley Road King.* So we head off, getting some footage of me doing my best Born to be Wild impression. But after about half an hour, we realise we're lost.

We're trying to find this industrial estate where their clubhouse is.

We eventually get to the clubhouse an hour and a half late and there's about seventy of these beautiful custom-made bikes, their chrome shining in the sun. And their patch is a US confederate hat on a skull on the Confederate flag. And in this bikie gang you've got people from all across the region – Australia and beyond, every sort of European ancestry, indigenous and Pacific islanders, and they're all gathering under the US Confederate flag. It was slightly surreal. I could never get over just how unpopular almost all of them would have

---

* The director for this film was the soundman in Papua New Guinea when we had guns pointed at us. I still tease him about the fact that in the footage it looks like he tries to blend into the background and hopes they don't notice him. As if a big white guy in the highlands of Papua New Guinea isn't going to stand out whatever he does (especially holding a sound boom).

been if they'd rocked up in the southern states during the Confederacy.*

And all the women that work behind the bar are topless. They're sitting outside on the kerb in their jeans, smoking cigarettes, asking, 'Where's the pom?' So then I arrive, feeling like Marlon Brando, though I'm reliably told I was more Wallace from *Wallace and Gromit*.

And their clubhouse is enormous, and absolutely immaculate inside. They invite us in, show us a huge amount of hospitality and explain how they feel they're being persecuted by law enforcement and the government. We meet two brothers: Shane and Dean Martin. These were tough men. Shane's bicep was pretty much as wide as my entire chest.

Then it's time to head out on the memorial tour. Everyone mounts up and the noise is just unbelievable. There's about seventy of them, all wearing Rebel jackets and German helmets. So we come out of the clubhouse and go straight through a red light with the police following us. And I can definitely see the appeal of being part of this powerful gang. It's certainly a notch up from riding my purple chopper around the close in Rainham.

We're not stopping at red lights, just driving right through. To be fair, people know we're coming. We sound like a swarm of bees the size of freight trains. I'm just starting to get used to being up front when I look down at my petrol gauge and see it's on red. What I can't do is to just leave the convoy without

---

* It's the same with gangs I've encountered in places like LA and New Zealand who have Nazi insignias. They really wouldn't have done very well under the actual Nazis, but so often it's more about sticking two fingers up at the establishment that they feel has turned their back on them, And nothing does that like some Nazi iconography, even though Hitler probably wouldn't have been their biggest fan.

explaining why. But it's so noisy, I can't call out. I weigh up which option is the least bad and decide that anything is better than running out of petrol and trundling to a halt. So I manage to get Shane's attention and mime that I need to stop for petrol.* At the next petrol station, I pull in and Dean puts his arm out and the whole convoy stops while I put petrol in my bike. I am very conscious of all those eyes watching me. I've never known a petrol tank to fill as slowly in my life. Not only did Wallace arrive an hour and a half late, he's also wasting the time of men whose time you do not waste. These are men with the capacity to be pretty scary, but they all sit patiently while I fill the tank. Eventually we make it to the graveyard, for the whisky and the weed and the poetry, and it's a very emotional thing. It was a genuine honour to be there. Then we ride all the way back to their clubhouse and the party starts. They're incredibly hospitable and definitely know how to throw a party.

As I have been many times in my life, I was very grateful to my friend Jarrod Gilbert for the connections that got us into the Rebels. Or Dr Jarrod Gilbert, to give him his full title. He is an expert, amongst many other things, on the various gangs of New Zealand and has written the definitive account, *Patched*. Contrary to the popular belief that New Zealand is only sheep, the All Blacks and Bilbo Baggins, there are more gangs per capita in New Zealand than any other country on the planet. Some of the funniest times of my life have been spent with Jarrod. He's one of my closest friends and he is a surprising mix of things. He once knocked out a massive bloke in Papua New Guinea who tried to rob us. If you're looking for a man to accompany you around the world, a professor of sociology

---

* Don't ever let them tell you a qualification in mime is good for nothing.

with a mean right hook and a wicked sense of humour is as good a combination as I've ever encountered.

I'd been with Jarrod ten years previously with a different group of very tough men, when we'd been making a film about a gang known as the Mongrel Mob, who are still the biggest gang in New Zealand. They'd formed in the sixties, when a judge had called a group of young men 'mongrels' and they said they'd decided to be what society told them they were. I got to know one of their spokesmen called Dennis pretty well on that trip.

Dennis is a very tough man. He's huge, with a mask of facial tattoos. He's Samoan and he had from his stomach down to his thighs marked with traditional Samoan tribal tattoos. And I'm reliably informed the tattoos go *everywhere*. They're done the traditional way with spit and charcoal and sharpened whalebone they hit with a wooden mallet. You're supposed to have them done gradually over a series of months, so you can recover from the pain. But Dennis had them done in one weekend.

He is also a man who walked into a police station and challenged every man in there single-handed. The reports were that it was a draw. Earlier in the day, we'd gone to a rugby league match between the North and South Island Mongrel Mob. There were no boots with studs, just Doc Martens* and bare feet. When we'd first arrived, we'd been told in no uncertain terms to go away, even though I'd told them in an only slightly squeaky voice that we were 'friends of Dennis'.

After the game and the subsequent party, we picked up Dennis to drive through the night to our next location. Jarrod is driving us through the beautiful South Island New Zealand

---

* There was no one there from Basildon.

259

countryside in a camper van. Dennis is a bit worse for wear and decides to sleep in one of the bunks, which is up on a shelf above the driver's seat. Jarrod and I are talking nonsense, making each other laugh. Dennis is snoring like an industrial wood saw above us. And I'm not sure what happens next, but Jarrod must have seen something, or thought he saw something he wanted to avoid, or perhaps aim for. Suddenly we're on the wrong side of the road just as an absolutely enormous sheep truck is coming towards us, so Jarrod veers off road for a bit and then when he veers back on, there's a big bump and Dennis goes flying through the air.

My first thought is that Dennis might be hurt. The second is that he might not be very happy with what has just happened, and Dennis isn't the sort of bloke you want to have unhappy. We pull over and look in the back, to find Dennis fast asleep on the sofa. He has fallen seven feet out of a bed, somehow missing the box of beers, the sink and the gas hob, and landed safe on the sofa without even noticing. He's still snoring gently like a baby. He never knew that he'd fallen asleep in the top bunk and woken up on the sofa. If you're reading, Dennis, sorry.

La Dolce Mitchell

'What's sorry in Italian?' I whisper out of the side of my mouth to Steve. The driver they'd sent to meet us is not pleased. Not pleased at all. The Mitchell brothers are on tour and we've already upset someone.

Cindy Beale had taken the kids and gone to Italy. Even though Phil and Grant were Ian's mortal enemies, Cathy had convinced them to get over there and sort it out. So this meant filming a special on location on Lake Como in Italy. Steve and I had been filming in the morning and flew out separately from the others and had a couple of beers on the flight over.

When we arrived at Milan airport, there was a bloke holding a sign up saying 'Steve McFud' and 'Kempo Rossa'. Well, we say, that's not us, so we should go to the bar and wait for whoever is picking us up. There were a load of people from a motorbike show in there and Steve is massively into his bikes, so we were talking to these guys, and they were buying us drinks, and we're buying them back and we totally lost track of the time. And then I see this guy with the sign wandering past and I look at my watch and it's been three hours or something and so we're both like, 'We'd better go.' So we go and introduce ourselves to him and he's a bit annoyed, which is fair enough.

'You have been here long time,' he says accusingly. And we slur back. 'Yess, yess we have.'

We get in the car, and we drive to Lake Como, and it must have been the best part of two hours. We get to this beautiful hotel on the shore of Lake Como, which is going to be used as a location, so we're all staying there. I was still very into my fashion back then, so I'm wearing this long Gucci leather coat and Gucci loafers. Whereas Steve is in holiday mode, wearing shorts and a Fred Perry T-shirt and trainers. We rock up in the reception and there's a violinist and a cellist and a pianist and they're playing classical music. Marble and chandeliers. And these kind of very neat, Italian-Austrian-style guys on reception. Neat moustaches and neat hair, who literally click their heels.*

So we're having a couple of beers again and one of these guys comes up to us and says, 'I'm afraid the signori cannot be here in shorts.'

Steve puts his beer down and stands up. 'So it's the shorts that's the problem,' he says, looking this bloke in the eye. 'Are you saying you don't like my shorts?' And then he reaches very obviously towards his waistband, looking him in the eye the whole time. Like a Mexican stand-off. I swear the violinist even stops playing. There's silence. Eventually, the waiter obviously realises that Steve is not bluffing and he backs down and says, 'Please enjoy your drink, signori.' And that set the tone for Phil and Grant in Italy.

---

* It was the kind of place that sold bottles of wine with a picture of Mussolini on the label.

Gazza

Six years after he famously cried in Italy, Paul Gascoigne and I are being driven down the M40, standing up and waving at each other through the sun roofs of our cars.

I am thirty-two years old, and Grant Mitchell has just got together with Tiffany from the Queen Vic. I don't know it yet, but our storylines will go on to be watched by more than twenty million people. Me and Gazza are coming down the motorway from playing croquet outside an exclusive country hotel and have decided that the thing to do is to find somewhere to have something to eat. I had gotten to know him pretty well over the previous couple of years.* He is one of the kindest, funniest, nicest men I've ever met. He came from real poverty and dragged himself up through his talent and hard work. He is incredibly funny and cleverer than people give him credit for. He's also extremely kind and generous. You see how loved he is when you go out and about with him. I went out in Glasgow with Gazza when he played for Rangers and I've never seen anything like it. He couldn't move two feet without someone buying him a drink.

So a few weeks after the agony of that final defeat to Germany, we decide to drown our sorrows together.

---

* If you Google search 'Ross Kemp + Gazza' now, Google will prompt you, 'Do you mean Ross Kemp + Gaza?'.

As we leave the hotel, one of the French women who worked there says, in French, 'Thank God they're leaving.' And my girlfriend at the time replies, in fluent French, 'I couldn't agree more.'

When we get to the restaurant, which is famous for having a stream running through the middle of it, we're crossing the bridge and Gazza falls in. Then, as I try and pull him out, I fall in too. As we sit dripping at our table, apologising but unable to speak because we're laughing so hard and wiping each other with napkins, someone asks us if we want water for the table and it sets us off again.

A couple of days later, a paper put out a photo of us all with a caption saying, 'Just goes to show that money can't buy class.' It can't. But it can buy you an extremely fun day out.

A Perfect Night Out

There's a saying that you should never meet your heroes or your celebrity crushes. I strongly disagree. You should definitely have a very fun night with someone you fancied when you were a teenage boy.

I was sat at the roof terrace of a bar one evening with a friend who I've filmed with around the world after we'd had a meeting with some producers. They'd left and my friend and I had stayed there as the sun went down. The sound of the city all around us. We'd started on beers and by this point we were onto rosé. We were reminiscing about the ridiculous things that had happened to us, when I became aware that there was a bit of a fuss at one side of the bar, and people were taking selfies. There was a woman in the middle of all the fuss and, at first, I thought she was someone I knew. But quite quickly realised who she was. I'd had a poster of her and her group on my bedroom wall in my late teens. As the evening went on, and my friend and I drank more rosé and told more stories, everyone moved about and I found myself sitting next to her. I caught her eye and smiled and leaned in to say something and then we started kissing. We were well above the age of smooching in the back row of a cinema. But that's very much what it was like. Then we laughed.

'It's you,' she said. And I nodded and said, 'it's you.' Then we started talking. My friend was getting on well with her friend and we ordered a bottle of wine. Then another bottle of wine. It was one of those moments when you just click with someone and it's as if you've known each other for a long time. That feeling that you could go on talking forever. It was a hot summer evening, and we were sat outside at a rooftop bar in Soho. We fell down the stairs at the end of the night.

We were never in touch again. I'm not sure why from her point of view. I think, from mine, it felt like one of those things that should be left as it was. If we'd met up again and it was awkward or stilted or not like that night, it would have ruined the memory.

We didn't even have breakfast.

Worst Breakfast Ever

No one ever wants their breakfast to have claws. I'm not a fussy eater and I've always tried to be non-judgemental about food, after all what's normal entirely depends on your context. For some people, bush meat is a delicacy, for others a necessity, for me it's something I have never touched. But that morning when they set down a skillet in front of us, it was a primate that had been cut into quarters and a whole porcupine – you could still see its claws and its little face.

I was on the trip to Democratic Republic of Congo where I had met Dr Mukwege, the Nobel-Prize-Winning surgeon, and we ended up staying out in the jungle. We'd got on a UN helicopter out there to see where some of the fiercest fighting was. And we're in a place controlled by rebel soldiers. They're wearing berets and camouflage gear, they're carrying AK-47s and grenades, but on their feet they're wearing these bright white wellington boots. It'd been a particularly rough night, laying on a mattress and being eaten by bedbugs and mosquitos, and at one point two men burst into my room wanting a can of beef that did not exist, shouting 'Où est le bœuf, où est le bœuf?' I managed to fend them off with a penknife, a torch and my appalling French. They'd spent most of the night in the bar below with the rebel soldiers, watching *Black Hawk Down*, which for them involved cheering every time an American soldier got shot. And, as it happens a lot when you're from the UK, I was pretty sure they would just assume we were Americans.

I got through the night with no sleep whatsoever, dehydrated, too scared to go to the toilet, so I weed in a little plastic bottle. I was exhausted and starving. And then we got downstairs and breakfast arrived. But there was no way I was going to eat a breakfast that had a face.

DRC was a deeply unsettling place. We had driven across the border from Rwanda and you wouldn't have realised you were now in DRC, except for the fact that suddenly there was plastic waste everywhere. Rwanda has banned plastic bags and is very hard-line about enforcing it. People ride about on these wooden half-bike, half-scooters called 'chukudus', which look like they've been jerry-rigged from anything they could find. You see them piled high with cargo on every street.

That day we went to film with another group called the Mai Mai, who not only believed that certain herbs made you impervious to bullets but also wanted to sing us a song.

We asked our fixer to explain what they were singing, and he told us it was: 'The white man's filming us, but we're filming him. Yes, we are. He thinks he's filming us, but we're filming him.' That's how it was translated to us at the time and what the subtitles said when it was broadcast.

A week after it went out on TV, we got a call from someone who spoke the local dialect who told us that what they had actually been singing was: 'The white man shagged us all night, never paid us a thing. No he didn't. He shagged us all night and never paid a thing.'

Call Me Dave

Big Dave. Dave Williams. Dave Sound. I've been through some of my scariest and funniest moments with him next to me (often him recording the barely intelligible things I'm saying in response). But I never thought I'd hire a room in a sex hotel with Big Dave.

I've worked with Dave for more than fifteen years and he's one of my closest mates. Over that period there have been different directors and camera people but Big Dave has been a constant. One thing you need to know about Dave is that he gets very annoyed whenever anyone we're interviewing doesn't want to use their real name – which often means they're up to no good, or of slightly dubious character – and the fake name they choose for themselves often tends to be Dave. So many of the worst people on the planet: rapists, terrorists, murderers: 'Call me Dave.'

We were once recording an interview with a guy who ran a chop house for the cartels, only not to chop up drugs. He was the guy they sent in when they wanted to find out where the money or drugs you'd stolen from them was. And he was the guy who disposed of what was left of you when he'd finished asking.

We arranged to meet him in Bonaventura, in a sex hotel, as you do.* When he arrives, he's in his early twenties, covered

---

* They are an excellent place to meet someone anonymously, as they have two separate garages and entrances.

in religious jewellery. And we start doing the interview, which we'll be doing in silhouette and with disguised voice, so as not to give his identity away. Dave says we have to turn off the air conditioning because it's too noisy. Now I'm not sure what kind of luxury sex hotels you're used to but this one was pretty rough. PVC furniture, all in shapes that bodies can fit over. And as I'm interviewing him, it's getting hotter and hotter. And what becomes apparent is that the air-conditioned temperature must have been keeping the lube solid. But as the temperature rises, it all starts to become liquid. And it is everywhere. There are handprints on every surface. And I'm dripping with sweat and John, the cameraman, is dripping with sweat. Dave Sound is dripping with sweat. The only dry thing in the entire place is the guy we're interviewing; not a single bead of sweat rolls down the side of his face. He tells how he would start with fingers, then one eye, leaving you with one to see what was going to happen next. The only problem was, they'd occasionally pick the wrong person, and that person would then not be able to answer his questions. And he tells us that his father was chopped up, how he once had to chop up his best friend. How his brother was chopped up by mistake because they thought it was him. He did this work because it was the only way he could stay alive. He was racked with regret and guilt.

There's a fridge in the corner with lube and condoms and sex toys, and bizarrely, a comb, which I'm not sure if it's always there, or whether they've put it there to mock me specifically. This interview takes about three hours. Marta is there directing and translating for us. The cameraman Johnathan is sitting on a large plastic camera case to give his legs a break but there's so much melted lube on the floor it has become like an ice rink. He slips and all fifteen stone of him, and the case, hit the lube rink with a bang that sounds like a rifle shot. We all jump. But not the guy we're interviewing. He barely moves. He's telling us, in a flat, matter-of-fact way, how he completely dismembers people in the hope they won't come back and haunt him. For him it's just part of a day's work.

After hearing some of the darkest things I've ever heard, we finish the interview and he's putting his crosses and rosaries back on. I ask him if he believes in God. And he says, 'I believe in God, but somehow I don't think I'm going to heaven.' At the end, I give him a release form and when I see what he's written for his name I take it straight over to Big Dave. 'Oh, come on,' he says.

On Falkland Road

'What's your name?' asks the man, who has clearly painted on his side-parted hair, complete with a quiff, with boot polish. In the heat of the Mumbai night, it has started to drip down the sides of his face. Our fixer, Nandan, and I are on Falkland Road, the most famous roads for prostitution in Mumbai.

'Tell him he can call me Dave,' I tell Nandan.

It's 2017 and I am on the trail of men and women who sell children into prostitution. Mumbai, population 20 million, is one of the world's busiest commercial centres. India is home to the largest sex industry in the whole of Asia. The scale is almost incomprehensible. Some estimate as many as 100 million people are involved across the whole of India: 10 per cent of the population.

We had seen how wary of the camera the old women who worked as pimps and madams were. Our rather diminutive director had already been hit over the head repeatedly with their sandals. Prostitution is legal, but there was still a huge stigma attached to it. When we had travelled to one of the less prominent red-light districts, barely anyone would speak to us. The young girls especially. We spoke to one woman who had been trafficked thirty-five years before, who told us that she had one girl who worked for her. This was a poor area of houses made of soft brick, many with corrugated iron roofs. The sex workers here were for poorer, working-class customers.

One of the girls we did speak to said she didn't know how old she was. Another girl I spoke to, who had physical and mental disabilities, had already been sold to six men that night, at twenty-three pence a time. Later, people started running, fear in the air. It was a stampede, and we had caused it just with our presence because both of my 6ft-plus crew members were wearing head torches and, to the locals, looked like something from outer space. The pimps were unhappy that we were disrupting their business. So we left.

We wanted to try and find out where the girls who were trafficked by people like Mr Khan ended up. We had heard stories that brothel owners were injecting chicken growth hormone into girls' breasts to make them look older. I'd got used to hearing terrible things over the years but there are some things that cause you to pause. To try and understand what has happened to people that they can put aside their natural instinct to care for children and instead trap them and send them into an environment like this. So we wanted to find evidence of these girls ending up in brothels on Falkland Road. Back in the colonial days, girls on the street would be kept in cages. There were no cages now, but there may as well have been.

I'm there playing the drunk sex tourist. Nandan our fixer is with me and he's a local journalist so he's going to play the role of the local guy I've paid to try and get me young girls. I've said I want twelve at the oldest. And we've got these little hidden cameras on us. I can very rarely do much undercover stuff in our films. But we've decided in this place it will work. It's evening, still very hot and humid, and the camera lenses are in the bottom buttons of our polo shirts. It downloads the footage onto a drive that you can then plug into a computer and watch. And there's a button. You push it once and it starts recording. Then you push it again and it stops recording. We practise a few times and then we're off.

We cross over the busy streets thronged with cars, mopeds and tuk-tuks. We walk down an alley into the red-light zone. And this street is several miles long with a mixture of bars and brothels with blokes hanging around outside.* I'm playing pretty pissed by now and we walk up and immediately these two guys – one of them boot-polish hair guy – start talking to us, asking if we want girls.

I'm holding a beer and we start following various blokes into brothels. And we keep saying, 'No, we need younger.' These pimps are clearly excited because there's the promise of money if they can find girls who are young enough. We must have gone into more than twenty brothels. We're playing it full on and I'm telling Nandan off because the girls aren't young enough and he's apologising. And the two pimps eventually take us to a place where they bring out these girls, and they are children, but they've clearly had the growth hormones injected because it's not natural for kids that young to look like that. I am sick to my stomach. And we've got the footage, so we make our excuses and leave. They seem disappointed that they didn't do their job well enough.

And even though we're doing this to try and draw attention to the situation, the whole thing has left us deeply affected by what we've seen. We walk back down this mile-long road, Nandan and I, in silence. We get back and Dave the sound man

---

* Just outside one of the slums we found a McDonald's, which everyone was very excited about. I went down an alleyway to do some walking shots, where what I thought was a cat started rubbing its head and body against me. Then I realised it was a rat. It had clearly been supersized by eating fast food.

274

and Jonathan the cameraman have been out having a delicious meal and they ask, 'How was it?' I just look at them. Then we plug the drives into the laptop and expectantly we wait for the footage to upload. Mine first. We press play. Nothing. On to Nandan's, we press play. Nothing on his either. We thought we'd turned our cameras on, but we'd turned them off. The entire five hours had been for nothing.

The camera may not have recorded it, but it was still burned into my brain. The next night, we had to go back to that place and do it all over again.

That trip was years before my daughters were born. I have never felt that the only way you can have empathy for your fellow humans is to have children. But it's definitely true that certain subjects hit differently when you have kids. When you travel around the world and see how little a life can be worth.

I was having a meal with Dave at the end of the trip and talking about what we'd seen. I was telling him more about my double act with Nandan. How I'd gone deep cover.

'So did you have a fake name?' asked Dave, looking at me carefully. And I just winked at him.

'Oh, you've got to be kidding me,' he said.

The Kemp Effect

'You've got to be kidding me,' says the police officer in his broad West Country accent when I take off my mask. 'I might have known it was you.' I get that a lot.

I've made over a hundred and twenty documentaries so far, in some of the roughest places in the world, and an unexpected consequence of that is that now people assume, if I'm somewhere making a doc, it must be *because* it's rough.

It was 2020 and we'd managed to get permission from the government to travel during lockdown to make a documentary about dementia for ITV, interviewing people who had to sell their parents' house to pay for their care due to dementia. Because in the UK it's seen as a social care issue, so it's effectively the families who are responsible for using any assets to pay for their relative's care.

Like many, this particular woman's mother had become quite physical as her dementia had progressed, and was having to be moved to a different home – and bear in mind this was during the middle of the pandemic. The mother had lived in this bungalow by the sea in Devon for years. Johnny, James and I, the crew, had driven down the night before and were staying in an Airbnb nearby. In a weird coincidence, the daughter of the woman with dementia had taught Johnny when he was a kid.

In the morning, we drive down into the village. On our way to do the interview, we stop off for breakfast. We've got masks and gloves on and I go to the garage counter with our pasties. As soon as I've paid, the woman behind the counter starts questioning me, 'What are you doing here?' And I explain that we've got permission to make a documentary. 'About who? What you doing here? Who are you?'

After getting out my press card and being very polite, we leave, and her husband gets into a car and follows us the whole way to where we're filming. And then he drives slowly past us.

We've brought a metal tape measure to make sure we're a safe distance apart, which we also have to film as evidence. We've just started having a chat with the woman over a cup of tea when a policeman turns up. And he starts asking us, 'What you doing here?'

We're outside, so I take my mask off and he says, in this broad West Country accent, 'Oh, I might have known it was you.'

I just smile as a hello.

'So, what you doing here?'

'We have permission, we can show you the paperwork.'

'How long you gonna be here?'

I explained that it's hard to say for sure because we haven't started to film yet, but we need to be back up to London that same day, so till five at the latest. 'Let's say five to five,' I say. 'Is that precise enough?'

We end up leaving at about ten to, and as we're leaving the village, there he is, coming down the other way. Doesn't acknowledge us or wave.

Before we left, we couldn't resist going back to the garage and buying the last of the pasties. She wasn't very happy to see us. These were clearly local pasties for local people.

Another time, I was in a run-down area. It was dark stuff, we were making a film about child sexual exploitation in a very deprived area of the UK. I was walking through the streets, interviewing an ex-gang member, when I became aware of a posse forming behind us. At a break in filming, a woman came up to us and explained that we needed to leave as it was going to impact the house prices. It was proper villagers-with-pitchforks stuff. This isn't the first time this has happened to me.

There's probably a racket to be had in turning up to posh areas and saying to people, 'Lovely village you've got here. It would be a real shame if someone were to make a hard-hitting documentary and tank the house prices.'

Realisation

If I was given the chance to relive one moment from my life that wasn't the birth of my children, it would be this one.

I was staying in the Al Maha Hotel in Dubai, in the desert. It was so hot during the day that you stayed in your luxury tent with air conditioning, a plunge pool and a bed big enough to play croquet on. I decide, as it was getting close to sunset, that I want to go horse riding (as you do). I'm not a great horse rider, but I hugely enjoy it whenever I get the chance. I'd already been for a bit of a ride a couple of days before.

I come into the stables and there are twelve beautiful Arab stallions. And one of them just stares at me with this look of challenge and it's literally like he's inviting me to step outside. The big South African guy who runs the stables sees me looking at him and says, 'Would you like to take him out?' And I very much would.

'He's a difficult horse,' he says. 'You be careful.'

I reach up and stroke the top of the horse's head and he responds and there's a connection. So I saddle up and I think because of the way I'd acted with the horse and how confident I was, the staff at that stable must think I'm a more competent rider than I am, because no one comes with me. And as I'm sat up on this massive horse, I'm suddenly struck by the fact that hacking across the Epsom Downs or pony trekking in

Wales might not be enough preparation for what I'm about to do. But here we go.

We trot out of the paddock and down this path. And he's pulling and pulling and I can tell he wants to go. When we're far enough from the stables, I take the handbrake off and whoosh. We're off. I've stood up out of the saddle and I've got my head down over his, whispering in his ear. I'm saying 'come on, come on'. We're pounding over the sand towards the dunes. He goes galloping up the dune, up to his forelocks and then at the crest, he locks his legs and we just slide down, with me leaning back. And then we go up another and slide down the other side again. I'd say at that moment it's about the most fun I'd ever had – it was like the realisation of every dream I'd had while riding my purple chopper round the streets of Essex. But the bigger realisation was still to come.

And even though the sun was setting behind us as we'd set off and I knew we had to head for home soon, I became aware of a weird glow ahead of us. As the sky got darker, the glow got brighter.

As we hit the top of the next dune, I see oil refineries lined up across the horizon down below us – the burn-off is lighting up the night sky, and it's like hell. Flames and thick black smoke. And in this moment it hit me how everything I'd been experiencing could only happen because of this. The air conditioning, the televisions, the swimming pools. All of it was because of this poisonous stuff hidden beneath the dunes. And I think that's when the true realisation happened, sitting on top of this horse, overlooking this inferno . . . that maybe saying other people's lines and pretending to be somebody else on TV* wasn't going to be enough for me. That I wanted

---

* Even though I enjoy it very much.

to look more deeply into the world around me. That there were other stories that needed to be told. That moment would change my life forever.

We trot back. He clearly knows his way home. But about half a mile away, his ears prick up and we're off again and we're hoofing it down this sandy path. When we get back, we get a strip torn off us by the stable manager. He comes running out, 'What do you think you're doing? You've upset every horse in the stable coming back like that.'

Apparently hearing us galloping back had set all the other horses off. Both of us look guiltily at each other. But both of us clearly thought it was worth it.

I will be eternally grateful to that horse for changing my life.

The Best Life Advice I Was Ever Given

When I was young, my father gave me a piece of advice: 'Don't worry about being happy all of the time, just try and find contentment.' I'm not sure if I knew what he meant back then. We all put so much store in looking for happiness. Contentment felt like settling for less somehow. I was young. Part of the process of growing up is making peace with the things you aren't going to be. You're not going to win an Oscar, you're not going to play on the wing for England at rugby, you're not going to win a Formula 1 Championship. Striving for happiness is always looking for the next thing. Contentment is making peace with who you are and what you have. To treat those you care about well. To have friends, to be able to look back and feel, on balance, you've done enough good things to make up for the bad. To love your family and to be loved. I used to worry what people thought about me for a large part of my life. But I don't worry about that anymore.

Partly, it's getting older. You look at yourself in the mirror enough times at my age and you lose any of that youthful regard for the surface of things. I don't care what people who don't know me say, because their opinion on who I am doesn't matter. More and more, I realise it's why I've been drawn to people whose relationships have been formed in extremity.

Because those relationships have been tested, there is something real at the centre of them. That laughter that comes from surviving contact with the enemy is partly chemical – your body doing something with the adrenaline and stress hormones. But it's also the laughter of relief, of joy at still being in the universe. You never forget that feeling and those you shared it with. I will take a grudging nod from a soldier I shared those experiences with over any other kind of praise.

I've been incredibly lucky that I've had a career as an actor, and that I've been able to make documentaries around the world. I hope that there are people who watched the documentaries and discovered something about other people's lives. It's not always been easy. My hearing has suffered. I regularly have to have things cauterised off me because no director ever asks you to film in the shade or wearing a sunhat. I've got a few scars, physical and mental. If I get run down, I get a flare-up of malaria.

But I have got to travel to almost* every continent, finding and telling stories. That's something I will never take for granted. And the thing about having no plan: you have to make peace with getting the things you want, but not necessarily in the order you want them.†

---

* If anyone wants to make a documentary about gangs of penguins, let me know.

† As I finished working on this book, the phone rang. 'What do you reckon about a trip to the prisons of Central and South America?' Looks like I won't be filling the dishwasher for a bit.

Picture Credits

All images are from the author's personal collection, except for the following:

Plate 2: © Mirrorpix *(top)*; © BBC *(bottom left)*; © Arthur Edwards/ The Sun/News Licensing *(bottom right)*

Plate 3: © Getty Images/Mark Thompson/ALLSPORT *(top)*

Plate 7: © Getty Images/Mark Cuthbert/UK Press *(top left)*

Acknowledgements

Firstly, my good friend, Scott Mitchell, who amongst many other things, came up with the title of this book. You're a good man.

To Jamie Coleman, for helping make this a book. To Vicky Eribo, Georgia Goodall and the rest of the team at Orion, for their expert editorial and publishing guidance. To my agent Alex Segal and the whole team at InterTalent.

Thank you to every teacher who helped me (you all have an incredibly difficult but important job).

Thank you to the cast and crew of *EastEnders* over the years.

My good friend and mentor, Lord Waheed Alli. My dear, departed friend Margaret McDonagh and to Clare Barton and Clive Tulloh for the endless support and advice over the years.

To everyone at the BBC, ITV, Sky, Tiger Aspect, STV, Honeybee, Sky History and Channel 5 who has helped me. I will always be eternally grateful for the opportunities I've been given. There are too many names to list them all, but you know who you are. Thank you.

To everyone who I've been lucky enough to work with making documentaries – I honestly believe that we have made a difference, maybe only a small one, but they were journeys worth making and we will carry on. Thank you from the bottom of my heart.

To every single fixer, journalist and contributor. Without you none of it would have been possible.

Thank you to the NHS, for allowing us to film and for looking after all of us, in particular the staff at John Radcliffe, for whom my family will always be eternally grateful.

To everyone in the Armed Forces who allowed me to see what you do and for your friendship. Thank you. To the Friday lunch club (you know who you are).

To the teams at Royal British Legion, Help for Heroes and Thames Hospice. Thank you.

To anyone I've missed out, it's a side effect of having too many people to be grateful to.

To my mum and my dad. To my talented brother and his family.

To Oliver, Leo, Ava and Kitty (and Bruno).

To my wife, Renée, for everything. I love you.

Credits

Seven Dials would like to thank everyone at Orion who worked on the publication of *Take Nothing for Granted*.

Agent
Alex Segal

Editor
Vicky Eribo

Editorial Management
Georgia Goodall

Editorial Assistant
Jane Hughes
Charlie Panayiotou
Lucy Bilton
Claire Boyle

Copy-editor
Anne O'Brien

Proofreader
Patrick McConnell

Audio
Paul Stark
Jake Alderson
Georgina Cutler

Contracts
Dan Herron
Ellie Bowker
Alyx Hurst

Images
Natalie Dawkins

Design
Nick Shah
Jessica Hart
Joanna Ridley
Helen Ewing

Finance
Nick Gibson
Jasdip Nandra
Sue Baker
Tom Costello

Inventory
Jo Jacobs
Dan Stevens

Production
Sarah Cook
Katie Horrocks

Marketing
Lindsay Terrell

Publicity
Virginia Woolstencroft
Becca Bryant

Sales
Jen Wilson
Victoria Laws
Esther Waters
Tolu Ayo-Ajala
Group Sales teams across
    Digital, Field, International
    and Non-Trade

Operations
Group Sales Operations team

Rights
Rebecca Folland
Tara Hiatt
Ben Fowler
Alice Cottrell
Ruth Blakemore
Ayesha Kinley
Marie Henckel